The Spirit Leads

The Spirit Leads

Margaret Fuller
in Her Own Words

Barry Andrews, Editor

Skinner House Books
Boston

Printed in the United States

Cover and text design by Suzanne Morgan.
Cover illustration provided by the James Smith Noel Collection, Noel Memorial Library, Louisiana State University in Shreveport.

ISBN 1-55896-565-3 / 978-1-55896-565-2

6 5 4 3 2 1 / 13 12 11 10

Library of Congress Cataloging-in-Publication Data

Fuller, Margaret.
The spirit leads : Margaret Fuller in her own words / Barry Andrews, editor.
    p. cm.
ISBN-13: 978-1-55896-565-2 (pbk. : alk. paper)
ISBN-10: 1-55896-565-3 (pbk. : alk. paper)
I. Andrews, Barry Maxwell. II. Title.
PS2502.A53 2010
818'.309—dc22
[B]

                        2010003819

Note: The Unitarian Universalist Association of Congregations is committed to using gender-inclusive language in its publications. However, in the interest of historical authenticity, quoted matter is printed in its original form.

We gratefully acknowledge permission to reprint the following materials:
"I am reminded…," fMS Am 1086 (1:91-95); "The advantages of…" fMS Am 1086 (1:197-201); "I am more…," fMS Am 1086 (1:13-17); I wish, if possible…," fMS Am 1086 (10:900); "The mere idealist…," bMS Am 1221 (216); "One day lives…," fMS Am 1086 (1:91-95); "Why should I not…," bMS Am 1569.7 (462); "We have just…," bMS Am 1280 (111:116-118); "For the past…," bMS Am 1280 (2358); "As to Transcendentalism…," bMS Am 1221 (209); "Mr. Emerson works…," fMS Am 1086 (9:71), fMS Am 1086 (2:635-641); "I had a…," bMS Am 1280 (2348), bMS Am 1280 (2383); Ms. Am. 1450 (72); "My dear friend…," bMS Am 1280 (2358); "I feel that…," fMS Am 1086 (9:91a); and "You say no secret…," fMS Am 1086 (9:170), bMS Am 1280 (111:213) reprinted with permission of Houghton Library, Harvard University.

"I am not…," Ms. Am. 1450 (103), bMS Am 1280 (111); "When I have been…," Ms. Am. 1450 (51); and "My love for…," Ms. Am. 1450 (109), Ms. Am. 1450 (115), Ms. Am. 1450 (58), reprinted courtesy of the Trustees of the Boston Public Library/Rare Books.

Margaret Fuller to James Freeman Clarke, 15 February 1843, Margaret Fuller Papers, Massachusetts Historical Society.

"It is Blossom Sunday…," reprinted by permission of the publisher from *The Journals and Miscellaneous Notebooks of Ralph Waldo Emerson: Volume XI, 1848–1851*, edited by A.W. Plumpstead, William H. Gilman, and Ruth H. Bennett, p. 469, Cambridge, Mass.: The Belknap Press of Harvard University Press, Copyright © 1975 by the President and Fellows of Harvard College.

This book is dedicated to my delightful granddaughter, Adelaide, in hopes that she, like Margaret Fuller, lives a life of extraordinary generous seeking.

—B.A.

Contents

Introduction

Religious radical, avant-garde cultural critic, feminist, progressive social theorist, investigative journalist, war correspondent, public intellectual — by any measure, Margaret Fuller was a remarkable person. She was a central figure in the Transcendentalist movement that included Ralph Waldo Emerson and many other close friends. And she applied her ideals to an active engagement with social change here in America and political revolution abroad. This year we celebrate the bicentennial of her birth. The readings chosen for this book are gleaned from the fullest extent of her works — her letters, her books and essays, her newspaper columns and dispatches, and the few portions of her journal that have made it into print. They reflect as well the fullest extent of her broad learning, her spiritual depth and her social concern.

I've organized these selections thematically, in eight sections, to encompass the breadth of Fuller's moral, religious, and social convictions, with the hope that they will give the reader a sense of the overall coherence of these spheres in her worldview. The quest for personal meaning and spiritual wholeness, self-reliance, a mystical connection to nature, a religious call to hopefulness and idealism, social justice, intellectual engagement, love and affection, and art and creativity were all inextricably linked for Fuller. Taken together, excerpts from her writings on each of these ideals create a picture of a woman who challenged herself and her contemporaries to constantly improve themselves and transform society.

Margaret Fuller was a pioneer in many ways, and yet she is as timely as ever. I hope that these brief passages will spark a curiosity to read more of her writings and learn more about her life. (The reader might begin with the list I have included at the end of this book.)

Although she was well known to the reading public in her own time, hers is hardly a household name today. The passage of years has dimmed her memory. Her tragic and premature death at the age of forty cut off what would surely have been continuing and substantial contributions to American society and culture. Unfortunately, her development and growing influence as a person and writer collided head on with her death in a shipwreck just a few hundred yards off of Fire Island in 1850.

Few now are familiar with her writing, even her groundbreaking feminist manifesto, *Woman in the Nineteenth Century*. But her work set the stage for women's liberation and shaped the tastes of the American public for art, music, and literature. In many respects, we have yet to catch up to her radical views on women, culture, and religion. They remain provocative and far-reaching even today.

This would not be surprising for anyone who knew her while she was alive or for those today who are familiar with the details of her life. Hers was a life of endless aspiration. In everything she applied herself to — writing, editing, education, social reform, and her own self-creation — Fuller aspired to grow and develop. This is what she wanted for herself, for others, for literature and art, and for her country. She chose as her motto a phrase by Goethe, her literary hero — "extraordinary generous seeking."

This seeking began early in life, when she was educated by her father, a cultured but stern disciplinarian. From a young age, she was tutored in the classics, reading Latin and studying English grammar by the time she was six. In her teens, she studied French and German and read widely among English and European authors. Her intellect was so highly stimulated that she suffered from nightmares and felt stifled in other areas of her development. "I look back on these glooms and terrors," she wrote, "and perceive that I had no natural childhood." Throughout the early years of her life, her soul was buried deep beneath the surface.

Nevertheless, under the influence first of Goethe and later Emerson, Fuller became a keen proponent of self-culture, the growth and development of the soul. Suffering under the weight of a patriarchal society that offered no outlet for her prodigious talents and depressed at the prospect that her gifts would go unrecognized, she experienced a breakthrough at the age of twenty-one.

She had gone to church so as not to displease her father, but felt suffocated by the service. As she put it, "I was wearied out with mental conflicts, and in a mood of . . . child-like sadness. I felt within myself great power, and generosity, and tenderness; but it seemed . . . as if they were all unrecognized, and . . . impossible that they should be used in life. I was only one-and-twenty; the past was worthless, the future hopeless." She fled the church as soon as the service was over, walking for miles across the bleak Thanksgiving landscape. At length, she paused by a stream and had a vision that released her pent-up soul. In a letter to a friend she wrote:

> I remembered how, a little child, I had stopped myself one day on the stairs, and asked, how came I here? How is it that I seem to be this Margaret Fuller? What does it mean? What shall I do about it? I remembered all the times and ways in which the same thought had returned. I saw how long it must be before the soul can learn to act under these limitations of time and space, and human nature; but I saw, also, that it Must do it, — that it must make all this false true, — and sow new and immortal plants in the garden of God; before it could return again. I saw there was no self; that selfishness was all folly, and the result of circumstance; that it was only because I thought self real that I suffered; that I had only to live in the idea of the All, and all was mine. This truth came to me, and I received it unhesitatingly; so that I was for that hour taken up into God. In that true ray most of the relations of earth seemed mere films, phenomena.

Though she continued to feel frustrated and unappreciated, Fuller's pain at not being recognized "never went deep" after this. She came to the conclusion that "the only object in life was to grow," in spite of all the obstacles she faced. "I was often false to this knowledge, in idolatries of particular objects, or impatient longings for happiness," she wrote to a close friend, "but I have never lost sight of it, have always been controlled by it, and this first gift of thought has never been superseded by a later love."

For someone so well educated and committed to the development of her fullest potential, Fuller pursued the one profession that was open to women of her talents — teaching. She assisted Bronson Alcott at his Temple School in Boston and taught for a time at the progressive Greene Street School in Providence, Rhode Island. Returning to Boston in 1839, she began conducting Conversations with women, a series of gatherings that continued for five years.

These Conversations were designed to promote the self-culture of women who had little encouragement and scant opportunity to pursue it on their own. They were facilitated discussions drawing on classical mythology and literary themes. These were not so much academic exercises as they were a means of raising consciousness among a large group of women otherwise relegated to limited and constricting domestic roles.

Fuller was the only regular female member of the Transcendentalist "club" that included Emerson and numerous other close friends, most of whom, like Fuller herself, were Unitarians. The Transcendentalists were religious radicals of a mystical bent, whose "new views" were considered heretical by orthodox Unitarians. At Emerson's urging, Fuller became editor of the *Dial* magazine, publishing articles, some of which she wrote herself, on religion, culture, and society, reflecting the Transcendentalist viewpoint. She used the experience to hone her skills as a writer and critic.

Her first major publication was *Summer on the Lakes*, an account of a trip to the Midwest with friends in 1843. Originally conceived as a conventional piece of travel literature, the book became an impassioned critique of the mistreatment of Native Americans and of the plight of women living in social isolation on the Great Plains. Returning to the East coast, Fuller accepted an offer from Horace Greeley to write for his newspaper, *The New York Daily Tribune*. In so doing, she became the first prominent woman columnist for an American newspaper, with a front page byline covering everything from reviews of books, plays, and concerts, to social criticism on topics such as the treatment of women prisoners, prejudice against immigrant groups, and American expansionism.

In 1845, Fuller published *Woman in the Nineteenth Century*, enlarging on an essay she had originally written for the *Dial* magazine. She had long felt oppressed by male dominance in society and the limited roles that women were allowed to occupy. Most professions were closed to women. They could not vote or own property. Their financial affairs were managed by men. They were regarded as inferior, like slaves, subject to the condescension and abuse of their male masters. "The lot of woman is sad," she wrote. "She is constituted to expect and need a happiness that cannot exist on earth. She must stifle such aspirations within her secret heart, and fit herself, as well as she can, for a life of resignations and consolations."

Fuller attacked male dominance head on. "We would have every arbitrary barrier thrown down," she insisted. "We would have every path laid open to woman as freely as to man. . . . What woman needs is not as a woman to act or rule, but as a nature to grow, as an intellect to discern, as a soul to live freely and unimpeded, to unfold such powers as were [innately] given her." Asked what offices they might fill, she famously replied, "Let them be sea-captains, if you will."

Appearing three years before the women's convention at Seneca Falls, New York, in 1848, Fuller's book had a tremendous impact on her feminist contemporaries. Elizabeth Cady Stanton and Susan B. Anthony said of Fuller that she "possessed more influence upon the thought of American women than any woman previous to her time." Challenging the social structures that kept women in servitude, envisioning a more harmonious and mutually enriching relationship between men and women, *Woman in the Nineteenth Century* was a radical and groundbreaking achievement.

Steeped as she was in European thought and literature, Fuller jumped at the chance to travel abroad as a governess to the child of a wealthy couple. She also arranged with Horace Greeley to cover the social and literary scene and send home dispatches on "Thoughts and Things in Europe." After brief stays in England, Scotland, and France, she arrived in Italy, where she felt most at home, and soon got caught up in the revolutionary fervor that was sweeping Europe in the late 1840s. The Italians, long divided and occupied by foreign powers, hoped to throw off foreign domination and achieve unification and independence.

Euphoria in the wake of early successes gave way later on to despair as the Austrians and then the French sought to put down the revolt. Fuller reported on these developments from Rome, which was besieged and then attacked by French troops. It was while in Rome that Fuller met a young Italian count, Giovanni Ossoli, fighting on the side of independence. They were secretly married and had a child, information they withheld from family and friends.

As the tide turned against the revolutionaries, Fuller took a more active part in the struggle herself. She left her son, Angelo, with a wet nurse in the mountains and joined her husband in Rome, managing a hospital flooded with wounded from the French attack. Her dispatches to Greeley's *Tribune* became more partisan and impassioned as Fuller herself took up the cause of Italian independence. When Rome fell, the Ossolis fled to Florence. From there, they embarked for America, meeting a tragic death in a shipwreck off the coast of Long Island. The whole family perished, and only young Angelo's body was ever recovered.

Margaret Fuller Ossoli was only forty years old. She had already accomplished a great deal in her short life, thanks in part to the head start she had been given by her demanding father. A memoir, taken from her letters and journals, was compiled by her friends Emerson, James Freeman Clarke, and William Henry Channing. We'll never know what might have been added to the account of her life had she returned safely.

From a very early age Fuller knew she "was not born to the common womanly lot" and would need to find her own way in life, "a pilgrim and sojourner on earth." Her deepest and most sustained relationship was with Emerson. And although it was a troubled one in many ways, she drew strength from his insistence on self-sufficiency. As she confided to her journal, "I must make my own path. . . . We need great energy, and self-reliance to endure to day. My age may not be the best, my position may be bad, my character ill-formed, but thou, Oh Spirit, hast no regard to aught but the seeking heart."

More than anything, Fuller was guided by mystical visions that came to her at pivotal moments in her life. "I was not without hours of deep spiritual insight and conscious of the inheritance of vast powers," she wrote. "I touched the secret of the universe, and by that touch was invested with talismanic power which has never left me, though it sometimes lies dormant for a long while." In these moments of vision, she saw that life goes on an "undulating" course, "sometimes on the hill, sometimes in the valley," and that the lesson of such insights was not to forget the hill-prospect when we find ourselves in the valley, to know in times of darkness that "the sun will rise again."

Although painfully aware that there was a great deal of "bitter mixed in the cup of life," she possessed a heroic optimism that never abandoned her. "I would beat with the living heart of the world," she announced. "Let me stand in my age with all its waters flowing round me. If they sometimes subdue, they must finally upbear me, for I seek the universal — and that must be the best."

Like her Transcendentalist friends, Fuller also had a progressive outlook on life. If existence is painful, if the world needs improving, patience and perseverance will make them right in the end. "I believe in Eternal Progression," she insisted. "I believe in a God, a Beauty and Perfection to which I am to strive all my life for assimilation. From these two articles of belief, I draw the rules by which I strive to regulate my life."

In Fuller's case, this striving for perfection manifested itself in a lifelong pursuit of self-culture, which for her meant the unfolding of our higher, spiritual nature. Her regimen — along the lines of the Transcendentalists generally — consisted of reading, contemplation, journal-writing, conversation, social activism, walks in nature, and periods of solitude. She did not seek social success, but an active, thoughtful life, always "seeking to be wise."

As a Transcendentalist, Fuller shared the group's aversion to materialism and commercialism on the grounds that they debase the spiritual life and contribute to social inequity. In a letter to a friend, she wrote: "Their hope for man is grounded on his destiny as an immortal soul, and not as a mere comfort-loving inhabitant of earth, or a subscriber to the social contract. It is not meant that the soul should cultivate the earth, but that the earth should educate and maintain the soul."

Religiously, Fuller was a mystic and a free-thinker. Like Emerson and the other Transcendentalists, she believed that religion cannot be received on external grounds but only on the basis of spiritual insight. Moreover, it must deal with the realities of this life, and not with hopes for the next one. "What is done here at home in my heart is my religion," she argued.

She maintained that, while the church is a human institution, founded on an impulse of the spirit, the spirit itself is "uncontainable and uncontained." It is constantly evolving in "an infinity of forms" — plants, animals, humans, stars, and other forms "not yet visible." It is in human beings that the soul has come to consciousness, but most people are not awakened and thus their purpose remains unrealized and unfulfilled. Judaism and Christianity represent one type of spiritual existence, but then, so does the Greek religion. In the progress of the spirit, new types will emerge and supersede the old.

Though most people seem to be in need of such institutions, Fuller could not abide them herself. Nowhere did she worship less, she said, than in the places set apart for the purpose. "The blue sky above the opposite roof preaches better" than any priest, because, at present, it represents "a freer, simpler medium of religion." She proposed that "When great souls arise again that dare to be entirely free, yet are humble, gentle, and patient, I will listen, if they wish to speak. But that time is not nigh."

Fuller's post-Christian spirituality set her apart from most of her fellow Transcendentalists, a number of whom were or had been Unitarian ministers. Her beliefs — which she set down in "A Credo" — were censored by editors, including Emerson, who thought they were too radical and provocative. (Even today it is difficult to find an unexpurgated version of that essay.) She was a spiritually well-grounded woman who felt free to express her own views on religion. On the one hand, as a lay person she did not feel constrained, as the clergy did, to dress her views in Christian tropes. On the other, she felt the church was a patriarchal institution, whose ministers — entirely male — stifled the spirituality of women.

The patriarchy that Fuller criticized in the church, she found in society as a whole. With the industrial revolution came the cult of domesticity, in which women were relegated to roles subservient to men. The aspirations of women found scant expression in a society that valued them solely as wives and mothers. The church promoted and reinforced this view, and Fuller found little in Christian scripture to counter it.

In her famous Conversations with women in Boston, Fuller turned to classical mythology in search of empowering images of women. She developed her thoughts further in "The Great Lawsuit," an essay published in the *Dial* magazine. This essay was the genesis of her seminal work, *Woman in the Nineteenth Century*. Drawing on her study of classical mythology, Fuller proposed that the selfhood of women combined elements of two goddesses, Minerva and the Muse.

Minerva was the Roman name for Athena, the Greek goddess of wisdom and war. In Fuller's view, Minerva was an emblem of female agency and self-reliance, a virgin goddess beyond male control. What she meant by the Muse was female creativity, or, as she put it, "the unimpeded clearness of the intuitive powers which a perfectly truthful adherence to every admonition of the higher instincts would bring to a finely organized human being." Fuller envisioned a balance between these two aspects of woman's nature, but because the creative powers of the Muse were suppressed by male dominance, women needed to summon Minerva, the warrior within, to throw off their subjugation.

Men, too, are enslaved and therefore impeded in their own self-fulfillment by habit and social customs. Fuller argued that men and women possessed both masculine and feminine traits. "Male and female represent the two sides of the great radical dualism," she insisted. "But in fact they are perpetually passing into one another. . . . There is no wholly masculine man, no purely feminine woman." The self-fulfillment of women *and* men depended on achieving a balance in each between the qualities of both.

"The Sacred Marriage" was her image for the reconciliation of male and female opposites, the incorporation of the two halves of the psyche into one. "The time will come," she said, "when from the union of this tragic king and queen, shall be born a radiant sovereign self." True self-reliance depends upon the achievement of a harmony in which both the King and Queen might rule together in the human soul.

In Fuller's mind, individual self-fulfillment was linked to social transformation. In addition to the liberation of women, she sought to improve the condition of Native Americans, immigrants, female convicts, and the working poor. Commenting on the mistreatment of Native Americans, she wrote, "Of all these plague-spots there is none from which we feel such burning pain of shame and indignation, as from the conduct of this nation toward the Indians. Spoliation, aggression, falsehood of the blackest character, a hundred times repeated, each time with increased shamelessness, mark every step of this intercourse."

In her more public role as a progressive social and cultural critic, Fuller sought to enlighten her fellow citizens and hold them to a higher moral standard. As she wrote in a *Tribune* column on New Years Day, "Can he sleep, who in the past year has wickedly or lightly committed acts calculated to injure the few or many. . . . If such sleep, dreadful shall be the waking."

Countering the anti-immigration sentiment of her day, she argued for multiculturalism. Ethnic groups, including the Irish and the Italians, contributed to the country's greatness, she insisted, and while they should be blended into "a new and generous" nation, their uniqueness must be preserved and appreciated. On issue after issue, from poverty to prisons, she believed her reading audience needed to undergo a personal transformation, liberating their minds from the inertia of prejudice and habitual thought, and awakening to the plight of society's victims.

Fuller's thinking was further enlarged as she was drawn into the struggle for Italian independence. This gave her a fresh perspective on problems at home and abroad. "Can I say our social laws are generally better, or show a nobler insight into the wants of man and woman," she asks:

> Then there is this horrible cancer of slavery, and the wicked war that has grown out of it. How dare I speak of these things here? I listen to the same arguments against the emancipation of Italy that are used against the emancipation of our blacks; the same arguments in favor of the spoliation of Poland, as for the conquest of Mexico. I find the cause of tyranny and wrong everywhere the same, — and lo! my country! the darkest offender, because with the least excuse; forsworn to the high calling with which she was called; no champion of the rights of men, but a robber and a jailer; the scourge hid behind her banner; her eyes fixed, not on the stars, but on the possessions of other men.

In spite of her deep disappointment in the failure of the Italian Revolution, she never surrendered her resolve or lost her idealism. Addressing her countrymen in one of her last dispatches from Rome following the French attack, she wrote, "Do you owe no tithe to Heaven for the privileges it has showered on you, for whose achievement so many here suffer and perish daily? Deserve to retain them, by helping your fellow men to acquire them. . . . Rest not supine in your easier lives, but remember 'Mankind is one, and beats with one great heart.'"

Even in defeat, Margaret Fuller was aspiring. She had struggled to overcome many obstacles in her own life. She championed the rights of women in a sexist and patriarchal society. She protested the treatment of oppressed and marginalized groups in America and fought for political liberty abroad. Through it all, she never lost faith in the progressive realization of her ideals. As she concluded her most famous and important work, "Always the soul says to us all: Cherish your best hopes as a faith, and abide by them in action. Such shall be the effectual fervent means to their fulfillment."

As we celebrate the bicentennial of this remarkable person, we might pause to reflect, not only on her many contributions to the life and thought of her own time, but also to consider the ways in which we might still find inspiration and guidance in her legacy today. Indeed, it might be asked, What can be said of the relevance of someone whom so few seem to remember?

Fuller's life was dedicated to a belief in Eternal Progression, not only of the self but also of society. Like her fellow Transcendentalists, she felt that personal transformation was a prerequisite for effective social change. She never ceased to appeal to the better nature of her readers or to a Higher Law that superseded even the Constitution and the Bible when these justified the institution of slavery, unjust war, and the subjugation of women.

For all our vaunted accomplishments as a nation and as a society, we seem to live in a more cynical time. Readers today may find Fuller's idealism somewhat naïve. But she herself was no stranger to suffering and oppression. She felt it in her own life and witnessed it in the lives of others. But she was able to draw from the deep well of a rich interior life, an education steeped in ancient wisdom as well as modern learning, and faith in a providential universe, the moral arc of which is long, but, in Theodore Parker's words, "bends toward justice."

Visitors to the Fuller family plot at Mount Auburn Cemetery in Cambridge, Massachusetts, will see a marker there to Margaret Fuller, but her body is missing. It was never recovered. Today, two hundred years after her birth, I believe we may yet reclaim what remains of her abiding and vital influence. We might well begin where she left off. Fuller was a gifted conversationalist who presided over a salon, as it were, engaging groups of women in conversations on a variety of topics. She was a strong believer in the use of conversation as a means of self-culture and social uplift. For her, neither personal transformation nor political change was accomplished alone; they both relied on group effort for success.

The selections in this volume were chosen because they are thought provoking and useful, not only for personal reflection but also as a springboard to group discussion. After her death, Fuller clubs sprang up across the country, inspired by Fuller's accomplishments and determined to carry on her work. Such clubs or circles might still be established for the same reason. In Unitarian Universalist congregations, for instance, discussion circles and study groups have been formed in recent years to explore and engage in the spiritual practice of the Transcendentalists, including Emerson and Thoreau.

Fuller shared in the spirituality of the Transcendentalists. Like Emerson, Thoreau, and the others, she was a religious seeker of the spiritual left. But she carried that viewpoint into a wider sphere of engagement and application than her Transcendentalist contemporaries. Like her, we might consider the ways in which our own spirituality — which owes so much to the Transcendentalists in our movement — might inform and influence our actions today. There is no better place to begin than reading and reflecting on the thoughts of Margaret Fuller.

Chronology

1810   Sarah Margaret Fuller is born in Cambridgeport, MA, May 23.

1823-24   Attends Prescotts' school in Groton, MA.

1824-33   Lives in Cambridge, MA. Friend of Henry Hedge, James Freeman Clarke, and William Henry Channing.

1833   Fuller family moves to a farm in Groton.

1835   Fuller's father, Timothy Fuller, dies suddenly, leaving her in charge of the family's finances.

1836   First visit to Emerson in Concord.

1836-37   Teaches at Bronson Alcott's Temple School in Boston.

1837-39   Teaches at Greene Street School in Providence, RI.

1839   Moves to Jamaica Plain, MA. Begins conducting Conversations with women in Boston and Cambridge (which continue until 1844).

1840   Edits the *Dial* from July of this year until July of 1842.

1841   Brook Farm begins. Fuller visits numerous times.

1843   Makes trip to the West with James and Sarah Clarke.

1844   *Summer on the Lakes* published. Moves to New York as literary critic for Horace Greeley's *New York Tribune*.

1845   *Woman in the Nineteenth Century* published.

1846   *Papers on Literature and Art* published. Sails for Europe. Travels in England, Scotland, and France.

1847   Arrives in Rome. Meets Giovanni Ossoli. Travels to Florence and Venice. Returns to Rome and resumes relationship with Ossoli.

1848   Spends the summer in the Abruzzi. Marries Ossoli, and gives birth to a son, Angelo, in September.

1849   Roman Republic proclaimed in February. Siege of Rome by the French. Fuller supervises a hospital.

1850   Leaves Rome for Florence. Sails for U.S. in May. Dies in a shipwreck off Fire Island, NY, on July 19, with her husband and child.

Our Pilgrimage Here

Margaret Fuller considered herself a pilgrim and a sojourner in life. Periods of loneliness, struggle, and personal crisis often culminated in moments of vision and spiritual insight when she felt in harmony with the universe and "conscious of the inheritance of vast powers." Fuller argued passionately that all human beings deserved the opportunity "as a nature to grow, as an intellect to discern, . . . to unfold such powers as were given."

Yet one word as to "the material," in man. Is it not the object of all philosophy, as well as of religion and poetry, to prevent its prevalence? Must not those who see most truly be ever making statements of the truth to combat this sluggishness, or worldliness? What else are sages, poets, preachers, born to do? Men go an undulating course, — sometimes on the hill, sometimes in the valley. But he only is in the right who in the valley forgets not the hill-prospect, and knows in darkness that the sun will rise again. That is the real life which is subordinated to, not merged in, the ideal; he is only wise who can bring the lowest act of his life into sympathy with its highest thought. And this I take to be the one only aim of our pilgrimage here. I agree with those who think that no true philosophy will try to ignore or annihilate the material part of man, but will rather seek to put it in its place, as servant and minister to the soul.

LETTERS, 1840

I rise a little before five, walk an hour, and then practise on the piano, till seven, when we breakfast. Next I read French, — Sismondi's Literature of the South of Europe, — till eight, then two or three lectures in Brown's Philosophy. About half-past nine I go to Mr. Perkins's school and study Greek till twelve, when, the school being dismissed, I recite, go home, and practise again till dinner, at two. Sometimes, if the conversation is very agreeable, I lounge for half an hour over the dessert, though rarely so lavish of time. Then, when I can, I read two hours in Italian, but I am often interrupted. At six, I walk, or take a drive. Before going to bed, I play or sing, for half an hour or so, to make all sleepy, and, about eleven, retire to write a little while in my journal, exercises on what I have read, or a series of characteristics which I am filling up according to advice. Thus, you see, I am learning Greek, and making acquaintance with metaphysics, and French and Italian literature.

"How," you will say, "can I believe that my indolent, fanciful, pleasure-loving pupil, perseveres in such a course?" I feel the power of industry growing every day, and, besides the all-powerful motive of ambition, and a new stimulus lately given through a friend. I have learned to believe that nothing, no! not perfection, is unattainable. I am determined on distinction, which formerly I thought to win at an easy rate; but now I see that long years of labor must be given to secure even the "*succes de societe*," — which, however, shall never content me. I see multitudes of examples of persons of genius, utterly deficient in grace and the power of pleasurable excitement. I wish to combine both. I know the obstacles in my way. I am wanting in that intuitive tact and polish, which nature has bestowed upon some, but which I must acquire. And, on the other hand, my powers of intellect, though sufficient, I suppose, are not well disciplined. Yet all such hindrances may be overcome by an ardent spirit.

LETTERS, 1825

I am reminded by what you say, of an era in my own existence; it is seven years bygone. For bitter months a treble weight had been pressing on me; the weight of deceived friendship, domestic discontent, and bootless love. I could not be much alone; a great burden of family cares pressed upon me; I was in the midst of society, and obliged to act my part there as well as I could. It was at the time I took up the study of German, and my progress was like the rebound of a string pressed almost to bursting. My mind being then in the highest state of action, heightened by intellectual appreciation, every pang, and Imagination, by prophetic power, gave to the painful present, all the weight of as painful a future.

At this time I never had any consolation, except in long, solitary walks, and my meditations then were so far aloof from common life that on my return, my fall was like that of the eagle which the sportsman's hand calls bleeding from his lofty flight to stain the earth with his blood.

In such hours we feel so noble, so full of love and bounty that we cannot conceive that any pain should have been needed to teach us. It then seems we are so born for good, that such means of leading us to it were wholly unnecessary. But I have lived to know that the secret of all things is pain and that Nature travaileth most painfully with her noblest product. I was not without hours of deep spiritual insight, and consciousness of the inheritance of vast powers. I touched the secret of the universe, and by that touch was invested with talismanic power which has never left me, though it sometimes lies dormant for a long while.

LETTERS, 1838

It is Blossom Sunday. The apple trees are full of blossoms, the golden willows too. I have found new walks, and a waterfall, and a pond with islands. But my feeling of beauty is superficial now, all these fair things are dumb compared with the last year. I long to feel them too. I feel near a faithful breast, yet gently put back by an irresistible power. I am like Ulysses near the loved shades . . . . It seems all mockery thus to play the artist with life, and dip the brush in one's own heart's blood. One would fain be no more an artist, or a philosopher, or a lover, or a critic, but a soul ever rushing forth in tides of genial life, or retiring evermore into precious crystals, too pure to be lonely. A life more intense, you say, we pine to have. But we mount the heights of our being, only to look down into darker colder chasms. It is all one earth, all under one heaven — but the moment — the moment.

LETTERS, 1839

3

The advantages of such a weekly meeting might be great enough to repay the trouble of attendance if they consisted only in supplying a point of union to well-educated and thinking women in a city which, with great pretensions to mental refinement, boasts at present nothing of the kind and where I have heard many of mature age wish for some such means of stimulus and cheer, and these people for a place where they could state their doubts and difficulties with hope of gaining aid from the experience or aspirations of others. And if my office were only to suggest topics which would lead to conversation of a better order than is usual at social meetings and to turn back the current when digressing into personalities or commonplaces so that — what is invaluable in the experience of each might be brought to bear upon all. I should think the object not unworthy of an effort. But my own ambition goes much farther. Thus to pass in review the departments of thought and knowledge and endeavor to place them in due relation to one another in our minds. To systematize thought and give a precision in which our sex are so deficient, chiefly, I think because they have so few inducements to test and classify what they receive. To ascertain what pursuits are best suited to us in our time and state of society, and how we may make best use of our means for building up the life of thought upon the life of action.

Could a circle be assembled in earnest desirous to answer the great questions. What were we born to do? How shall we do it? which so few ever propose to themselves 'till their best years are gone by. I should think the undertaking a noble one, and if my resources should prove sufficient to make me its moving spring, I should willing to give it a large portion of those coming years which will as I hope be my best.

LETTERS, 1839

It will not last. Many intricate labyrinths are yet to be traversed. Many caverns dark and cold shall be my prisons for a time but the crisis abodes on these broad sunny platforms with the commanding survey are unforgot. And of these broad marbles on which I rested for a while shall be built at last my temple, my palace home.

JOURNAL, 1844

In our own country, women are, in many respects, better situated than men. Good books are allowed, with more time to read them. They are not so early forced into the bustle of life, nor so weighed down by demands for outward success. The perpetual changes, incident to our society, make the blood circulate freely through the body politic, and, if not favorable at present to the grace and bloom of life, they are so to activity, resource, and would be to reflection, but for a low materialist tendency, from which the women are generally exempt in themselves, though its existence, among the men, has a tendency to repress their impulses and make them doubt their instincts, thus, often, paralyzing their action during the best years.

But they have time to think, and no traditions chain them, and few conventionalities compared with what must be met in other nations. There is no reason why they should not discover that the secrets of nature are open, the revelations of the spirit waiting for whoever will seek them. When the mind is once awakened to this consciousness, it will not be restrained by the habits of the past, but fly to seek the seeds of a heavenly future.

Their employments are more favorable to meditation than those of men.

Woman is not addressed religiously here, more than elsewhere. She is told she should be worthy to be the mother of a Washington, or the companion of some good man. But in many, many instances, she has already learnt that all bribes have the same flaw; that truth and good are to be sought solely for their own sakes.

WOMAN IN THE NINETEENTH CENTURY

I was taught Latin and English grammar at the same time, and began to read Latin at six years old, after which, for some years, I read it daily. In this branch of study, first by my father, and afterwards by a tutor, I was trained to quite a high degree of precision. I was expected to understand the mechanism of the language thoroughly, and in translating to give the thoughts in as few well-arranged words as possible, and without breaks or hesitation, — for with these my father had absolutely no patience . . . .

His influence on me was great, and opposed to the natural unfolding of my character, which was fervent, of strong grasp, and disposed to infatuation, and self-forgetfulness. He made the common prose world so present to me, that my natural bias was controlled. I did not go mad, as many would do, at being continually roused from my dreams. I had too much strength to be crushed, — and since I must put on the fetters, could not submit to let them impede my motions. My own world sank deep within, away from the surface of my life; in what I did and said I learned to have reference to other minds. But my true life was only the dearer that it was secluded and veiled over by a thick curtain of available intellect, and that course, but wearable stuff woven by the ages, — Common Sense.

AUTOBIOGRAPHICAL ROMANCE

It was Thanksgiving day, (Nov., 1831,) and I was obliged to go to church, or exceedingly displease my father. I almost always suffered much in church from a feeling of disunion with the hearers and dissent from the preacher; but to-day, more than ever before, the services jarred upon me from their grateful and joyful tone. I was wearied out with mental conflicts, and in a mood of most childish, child-like sadness. I felt within myself great power, and generosity, and tenderness; but it seemed to me as if they were all unrecognized, and as if it was impossible that they should be used in life. I was only one-and-twenty; the past was worthless, the future hopeless; yet I could not remember ever voluntarily to have done a wrong thing, and my aspiration seemed very high. I looked round the church, and envied all the little children; for I supposed they had parents who protected them, so that they could never know this strange anguish, this dread uncertainty. I knew not, then, that none could have any father but God. I knew not, that I was not the only lonely one, that I was not the selected Oedipus, the special victim of an iron law. I was in haste for all to be over, that I might get into the free air.

I walked away over the fields as fast as I could walk. This was my custom at that time, when I could no longer bear the weight of my feelings, and fix my attention on any pursuit; for I do believe I never voluntarily gave way to these thoughts one moment. The force I exerted

I think, even now, greater than I ever knew in any other character. But when I could bear myself no longer, I walked many hours, till the anguish was wearied out, and I returned in a state of prayer. To-day all seemed to have reached its height. It seemed as if I could never return to a world in which I had no place, — to the mockery of humanities. I could not act a part, nor seem to live any longer. It was a sad and sallow day of the late autumn. Slow processions of sad clouds were passing over a cold blue sky; the hues of earth were dull, and gray, and brown, with sickly struggles of late green here and there; sometimes a moaning gust of wind drove late, reluctant leaves across the path; — there was no life else. In the sweetness of my present peace, such days seem to me made to tell man the worst of his lot; but still that November wind can bring a chill of memory.

I paused beside a little stream, which I had envied in the merry fulness of its spring life. It was shrunken, voiceless, choked with withered leaves. I marvelled that it did not quite lose itself in the earth. There was no stay for me, and I went on and on, till I came to where the trees were thick about a little pool, dark and silent. I sat down there. I did not think; all was dark, and cold, and still. Suddenly the sun shone out with that transparent sweetness, like the last smile of a dying lover, which it will use when it has been unkind all a cold autumn day. And, even then, passed into my thought a beam from its true sun, from its native sphere, which has never since departed from me. I remembered how, a little child, I had stopped myself one day on the stairs, and asked, how came I here? How is it that I seem to be this Margaret Fuller? What does it mean? What shall I do about it? I remembered all the times and ways in which the same thought had returned. I saw how long it must be before the soul can learn to act under these limitations of time and space, and human nature; but I saw, also, that it MUST do it, — that it must make all this false true, — and sow new and immortal plants in the garden of God, before it could return again. I saw there was no self; that selfishness was all folly, and the result of circumstance; that it was only because I thought self real that I suffered; that I had only to live in the idea of the ALL, and all was mine. This truth came to me, and I received it unhesitatingly; so that I was for that hour taken up into God. In that true ray most of the relations of earth seemed mere films, phenomena.

7

My earthly pain at not being recognized never went deep after this hour. I had passed the extreme of passionate sorrow; and all check, all failure, all ignorance, have seemed temporary ever since. When I consider that this will be nine years ago next November, I am astonished that I have not gone on faster since; that I am not yet sufficiently purified to be taken back to God. Still, I did but touch then on the only haven of Insight. You know what I would say. I was dwelling in the ineffable, the unutterable. But the sun of earth set, and it grew dark around; the moment came for me to go. I had never been accustomed to walk alone at night, for my father was very strict on that subject, but now I had not one fear. When I came back, the moon was riding clear above the houses. I went into the churchyard, and there offered a prayer as holy, if not as deeply true, as any I know now; a prayer, which perhaps took form as the guardian angel of my life. If that word in the Bible, Selah, means what gray-headed old men think it does, when they read aloud, it should be written here, — Selah!

Since that day, I have never more been completely engaged in self; but the statue has been emerging, though slowly, from the block. Others may not see the promise even of its pure symmetry, but I do, and am learning to be patient. I shall be all human yet; and then the hour will come to leave humanity, and live always in the pure ray . . . .

Since then I have suffered, as I must suffer again, till all the complex be made simple, but I have never been in discord with the grand harmony.

MEMOIRS

A new page is turned, and an era begun, from which I am not yet sufficiently remote to describe it as I would. I have lived a life, if only in the music I have heard, and one development seemed to follow another therein, as if bound together by destiny, and all things were done for me. All minds, all scenes, have ministered to me. Nature has seemed an ever-open secret; the Divine, a sheltering love; truth, an always-springing fountain; and my soul more alone, and less lonely, more hopeful, patient, and, above all, more gentle and humble in its living. New minds have come to reveal themselves to me, though I do not wish it, for I feel myself inadequate to the ties already formed. I have not strength or time to meet the thoughts of those I love already. But these new have come with gifts too fair to be refused, and which have cheered my passive mind.

Apart, then, from good that is public and many-voiced, do not each of us know, in private experience, much to be thankful for? Not only the innocent and daily pleasures that we have prized according to our wisdom; of the sun and starry skies, the fields of green, or snow scarcely less beautiful, the loaf eaten with an appetite, the glow of labor, the gentle signs of common affection. But have not some, have not many of us cause to be thankful for enfranchisement from error or infatuation; a growth in knowledge of outward things, and instruction within the soul from a higher source. Have we not acquired a sense of more refined enjoyments; clear convictions; sometimes a serenity in which, as in the first days of June, all things grow, and the blossom gives place to fruit? Have we not been weaned from what was unfit for us, or unworthy our care? and have not those ties been drawn more close, and are not those objects seen more distinctly, which shall for ever be worthy the purest desires of our souls? Have we learned to do any thing, the humblest, in the service and by the spirit of the power which meaneth all things well? If so we may give thanks, and, perhaps, venture to offer our solicitations in behalf of those as yet less favored by circumstances. When even a few shall dare do so with the whole heart — for only a pure heart can "avail much" in such prayers — then all shall soon be well.

THANKSGIVING

Society is now so complex, that it is no longer possible to educate woman merely as woman; the tasks which come to her hand are so various, and so large a proportion of women are thrown entirely upon their own resources. I admit that this is not their state of perfect development; but it seems as if heaven, having so long issued its edict in poetry and religion, without securing intelligent obedience, now commanded the world in prose, to take a high and rational view. The lesson reads to me thus: —

Sex, like rank, wealth, beauty, or talent, is but an accident of birth. As you would not educate a soul to be an aristocrat, so do not to be a woman. A general regard to her usual sphere is dictated in the economy of nature. You need never enforce these provisions rigorously . . . . Express your views, men, of what you *seek* in woman: thus best do you give them laws. Learn, women, what you should *demand* of men: thus only can they become themselves. Turn both from the contemplation of what is merely phenomenal in your existence, to your permanent life as souls. Man, do not prescribe how the Divine shall display itself in woman. Woman, do not expect to see all of God in man. Fellow-pilgrims and helpmeets are ye, Apollo and Diana, twins of one heavenly birth, both beneficent, and both armed. Man, fear not to yield to woman's hand both the quiver and the lyre; for if her urn be filled with light, she will use both to the glory of God. There is but one doctrine for ye both and that is the doctrine of the SOUL.

MEMOIRS

The electrical, the magnetic element in woman has not been fairly brought out at any period. Every thing might be expected from it; she has far more of it than man. This is commonly expressed by saying that her intuitions are more rapid and more correct. You will often see men of high intellect absolutely stupid in regard to the atmospheric changes, the fine invisible links which connect the forms of life around them, while common women, if pure and modest, so that a vulgar self do not overshadow the mental eye, will seize and delineate these with unerring discrimination.

Women who combine this organization with creative genius, are very commonly unhappy at present. They see too much to act in conformity with those around them, and their quick impulses seem folly to those who do not discern the motives. This is an usual effect of the apparition of genius, whether in man or woman, but is more frequent with regard to the latter, because a harmony, an obvious order and self-restraining decorum, is most expected from her.

WOMAN IN THE NINETEENTH CENTURY

Whether much or little has been done or will be done, whether women will add to the talent of narration, the power of systematizing, whether they will carve marble, as well as draw and paint, is not important. But that it should be acknowledged that they have intellect which needs developing, that they should not be considered complete, if beings of affection and habit alone, is important.

Yet even this acknowledgment, rather conquered by woman than proffered by man, has been sullied by the usual selfishness. So much is said of women being better educated, that they may become better companions and mothers *for men*. They should be fit for such companionship, and we have mentioned, with satisfaction, instances where it has been established. Earth knows no fairer, holier relation than that of a mother. It is one which, rightly understood, must both promote and require the highest attainments. But a being of infinite scope must not be treated with an exclusive view to any one relation. Give the soul free course, let the organization, both of body and mind, be freely developed, and the being will be fit for any and every relation to which it may be called. The intellect, no more than the sense of hearing, is to be cultivated merely that she may be a more valuable companion to man, but because the Power who gave a power, by its mere existence, signifies that it must be brought out towards perfection.

WOMAN IN THE NINETEENTH CENTURY

Women are, indeed, the easy victims both of priest-craft and self-delusion, but this would not be, if the intellect was developed in proportion to the other powers. They would, then, have a regulator, and be more in equipoise, yet must retain the same nervous susceptibility, while their physical structure is such as it is.

It is with just that hope, that we welcome every thing that tends to strengthen the fibre and develop the nature on more sides. When the intellect and affections are in harmony; when intellectual consciousness is calm and deep; inspiration will not be confounded with fancy.

WOMAN IN THE NINETEENTH CENTURY

This author, beginning like the many in assault upon bad institutions, and external ills, yet deepening the experience through comparative freedom, sees at last, that the only efficient remedy must come from individual character. These bad institutions, indeed, it may always be replied, prevent individuals from forming good character, therefore we must remove them. Agreed, yet keep steadily the higher aim in view. Could you clear away all the bad forms of society, it is vain, unless the individual begin to be ready for better. There must be a parallel movement in these two branches of life. And all the rules left by Moses availed less to further the best life than the living example of one Messiah.

WOMAN IN THE NINETEENTH CENTURY

Were thought and feeling once so far elevated that man should esteem himself the brother and friend, but nowise the lord and tutor of woman, were he really bound with her in equal worship, arrangements as to function and employment would be of no consequence. What woman needs is not as a woman to act or rule, but as a nature to grow, as an intellect to discern, as a soul to live freely and unimpeded, to unfold such powers as were given her when we left our common home. If fewer talents were given her, yet if allowed the free and full employment of these, so that she may render back to the giver his own with usury, she will not complain; nay I dare to say she will bless and rejoice in her earthly birth-place, her earthly lot.

WOMAN IN THE NINETEENTH CENTURY

Thus is man still a stranger to his inheritance, still a pleader, still a pilgrim. Yet his happiness is secure in the end. And now, no more a glimmering consciousness, but assurance begins to be felt and spoken, that the highest ideal man can form of his own powers, is that which he is destined to attain. Whatever the soul knows how to seek, it cannot fail to obtain. This is the law and the prophets. Knock and it shall be opened, seek and ye shall find. It is demonstrated; it is a maxim. Man no longer paints his proper nature in some form and says, "Prometheus had it; it is God-like"; but "Man must have it; it is human." However disputed by many, however ignorantly used, or falsified by those who do receive it, the fact of an universal, unceasing revelation has been too clearly stated in words to be lost sight of in thought, and sermons preached from the text, "Be ye perfect," are the only sermons of a pervasive and deep-searching influence.

WOMAN IN THE NINETEENTH CENTURY

It is a time such as I always dreamed of; and that fire burns in the hearts of men around me which can keep me warm. Have I something to do here? or am I only to cheer on the warriors, and after write the history of their deeds? The first is all I have done yet, but many have blessed me for my sympathy, and blest me by the action it impelled.

My private fortunes are dark and tangled; my strength to govern them (perhaps that I am enervated by this climate) much diminished. I have thrown myself on God, and perhaps he will make my temporal state very tragical. I am more of a child than ever, and hate suffering more than ever, but suppose I shall live with it, if it must come.

LETTERS, 1848

I am not what I should be on this earth. I could not be.

My nature has need of profound and steadfast sentiment, without this I could have no steadfast greatness, no creative power.

I have been since we parted the object of great love from the noble and the humble. I have felt it towards both; yet a kind of chastened libertine I rove, pensively, always, in deep sadness, often O God help me; is all my cry. Yet I have very little faith in the paternal love, I need; the government of the earth does seem so ruthless or so negligent.

I am tired of seeing men err and bleed. I am tired of thinking, tired of hoping. I take an interest in some plans, *our* socialism, for instance, for it has become mine, too, but the interest is shallow as the plans. They are needed, they are even good, but man will still blunder and weep, as he has done for so many thousand years.

Coward and footsore, gladly would I creep into some green recess, apart from so much meddling and so much knowing, where I might see a few not unfriendly faces, where not more wretches would come than I could relieve.

Yes! I am weary, and faith soars and sings no more. Nothing is left good of me, except at the bottom of the heart, a melting tenderness. She loves much.

Thus I now die daily, and well understand the dejections of other troubled spirits with whom in times past I have communed.

LETTERS, 1849

Could we command enthusiasm; had we an interest with the gods which would light up those sacred fires at will, we should be even seraphic in our influences. But life, if not a complete waste of wearisome hours, must be checkered with them; and I find that just those very times, when I feel all glowing and radiant in the happiness of receiving and giving out again the divine fluid, are preludes to hours of languor, weariness, and paltry doubt . . . .

To this, all who have chosen or been chosen to a life of thought must submit. Yet I rejoice in my heritage. Should I venture to complain? Perhaps, if I were to reckon up the hours of bodily pain, those passed in society with which I could not coalesce, those of ineffectual endeavor to penetrate the secrets of nature and of art, or, worse still, to reproduce the beautiful in some way for myself, I should find they far outnumbered those of delightful sensation, of full and soothing thought, of gratified tastes and affections, and of proud hope. Yet these last, if few, how lovely, how rich in presage! None, who have known them, can in their worst estate fail to hope that they may be again upborne to higher, purer blue.

MEMOIRS

I am reminded to-day of the autumn hours at Jamaica Plain, where, after arranging everything for others that they wanted of me, I found myself, at last, alone in my still home, where everything, for once, reflected my feelings. It was so still, the air seemed full of spirits. How happy I was! with what sweet and solemn happiness! All things had tended to a crisis in me, and I was in a higher state, mentally and spiritually, than I ever was before or shall be again, till death shall introduce me to a new sphere. I purposed to spend the winter in study and self-collection, and to write constantly. I thought I should thus be induced to embody in beautiful forms all that lay in my mind, and that life would ripen into genius. But a very little while these fair hopes bloomed; and, since I was checked then, I do never expect to blossom forth on earth, and all postponements come naturally. At that time it seemed as if angels left me. Yet, now, I think they still are near.

MEMOIRS

If you saw me wholly, you would not, I think, feel as you do; for you would recognize the force, that regulates my life and tempers the ardor with an eventual calmness. You would see, too, that the more I take my flight in poetical enthusiasm, the stronger materials I bring back for my nest. Certainly I am nowise yet an angel; but neither am I an utterly weak woman, and far less a cold intellect. God is rarely afar off. Exquisite nature is all around. Life affords vicissitudes enough to try the energies of the human will. I can pray, I can act, I can learn, I can constantly immerse myself in the Divine Beauty. But I also need to love my fellow-men, and to meet the responsive glance of my spiritual kindred.

MEMOIRS

In the first place, the depth of the despair must be caused by the mistaken idea that this our present life is all the time allotted to man for the education of his nature for that state of consummation which is called heaven. Were it seen that this present is only one little link in the long chain of probations; were it felt that the Divine Justice is pledged to give the aspirations of the soul all the time they require for their fulfillment; were it recognized that disease, old age, and death are circumstances which can never touch the eternal youth of the spirit; that though the "plant man" grows more or less fair in hue and stature, according to the soil in which it is planted, yet the principle, which is the life of the plant, will not be defeated, but must scatter its seeds again and again, till it does at last come to perfect flower, — then would he, who is pausing to despair, realize that a new choice can *never* be too late, that false steps made in ignorance can never be counted by the All-Wise, and that, though a moment's delay against conviction is of incalculable weight, the mistakes of forty years are but as dust on the balance held by an unerring hand. Despair is for time, hope for eternity.

LETTERS, N.D.

I was now in the hands of teachers, who had not, since they came on the earth, put to themselves one intelligent question as to their business here. Good dispositions and employment for the heart gave a tone to all they said, which was pleasing, and not perverting. They, no doubt, injured those who accepted the husks they proffered for bread, and believed that exercise of memory was study, and to know what others knew, was the object of study. But to me this was all penetrable. I had known great living minds, — I had seen how they took their food and did their exercise, and what their objects were. *Very early I knew that the only object in life was to grow.* I was often false to this knowledge, in idolatries of particular objects, or impatient longings for happiness, but I have never lost sight of it, have always been controlled by it, and this first gift of thought has never been superseded by a later love.

MEMOIRS

Goethe, too, says he has known, in all his active, wise, and honored life, no four weeks of happiness. This teaches me on the other side; for, like Goethe, I have never given way to my feelings, but have lived active, thoughtful, seeking to be wise. Yet I have long days and weeks of heartache; and at those times, though I am busy every moment, and cultivate every pleasant feeling, and look always upwards to the pure ideal region, yet this ache is like a bodily wound, whose pain haunts even when it is not attended to, and disturbs the dreams of the patient who has fallen asleep from exhaustion.

MEMOIRS

Please, good Genius of my life, to make me very patient, resolute, gentle, while no less ardent; and after having tried me well, please present, at the end of some thousand years or so, a sphere of congenial and consecutive labors; of heart-felt, heart-filling wishes carried out into life on the instant; of aims obviously, inevitably proportioned to my highest nature. Sometime, in God's good time, let me live as swift and earnest as a flash of the eye. Meanwhile, let me gather force slowly, and drift along lazily, like yonder cloud, and be content to end in a few tears at last.

MEMOIRS

Italy has been glorious to me, and there have been hours in which I received the full benefit of the vision. In Rome, I have known some blessed, quiet days, when I could yield myself to be soothed and instructed by the great thoughts and memories of the place. But those days are swiftly passing. Soon I must begin to exert myself, for there is this incubus of the future, and none to help me, if I am not prudent to face it. So ridiculous, too, this mortal coil, — such small things!

I find how true was the lure that always drew me towards Europe. It was no false instinct that said I might here find an atmosphere to develop me in ways I need. Had I only come ten years earlier! Now my life must be a failure, so much strength has been wasted on abstractions, which only came because I grew not in the right soil. However, it is a less failure than with most others, and not worth thinking twice about. Heaven has room enough, and good chances in store, and I can live a great deal in the years that remain.

MEMOIRS

A Radiant Sovereign Self

In religious matters, Margaret Fuller was "a faithful skeptic," preferring to follow "the voice in the heart," rather than the preaching of the church. She rejected traditional Christianity for the reason that it rested on external grounds, which may lend life a formal decorum, but could never stir the depths of the soul. She was determined "to reject nothing but accept nothing till it is affirmed in the due order of mine own nature." Moreover, the Christian church promoted a patriarchy subordinating the spiritual life of women to that of men. Only when woman becomes religiously unfettered and self-reliant, Fuller said, could she achieve true equality and thereby develop "a radiant sovereign self."

Driven from home to home, as a Renouncer, I gain the poetry of each. Keys of gold, silver, iron, lead, are in my casket. Though no one loves me as I would be loved, I yet love many well enough to see into their eventual beauty. Meanwhile, I have no fetters, and when one perceives how others are bound in false relations, this surely should be regarded as a privilege. And so varied have been my sympathies, that this isolation will not, I trust, make me cold, ignorant, nor partial. My history presents much superficial, temporary tragedy. The Woman in me kneels and weeps in tender rapture; the Man in me rushes forth, but only to be baffled. Yet the time will come, when, from the union of this tragic king and queen, shall be born a radiant sovereign self.

MEMOIRS

Do you really believe there is anything "all-comprehending" but religion? Are not these distinctions imaginary? Must not the philosophy of every mind, or set of minds, be a system suited to guide them, and give a home where they can bring materials among which to accept, reject, and shape at pleasure? Novalis calls those, who harbor these ideas, "unbelievers"; but hard names make no difference. He says with disdain, "To *such*, philosophy is only a system which will spare them the trouble of reflecting." Now this is just my case. I *do* want a system which shall suffice to my character, and in whose applications I shall have faith . . . . I wish to arrive at that point where I can trust myself, and leave off saying, "It seems to me," and boldly feel, It *is* so to me. My character has got its natural regulator, my heart beats, my lips speak truth. I can walk alone, or offer my arm to a friend, or if I lean on another, it is not the debility of sickness, but only wayside weariness. This is the philosophy *I* want; this much would satisfy *me*.

LETTERS, 1833

I am more and more dissatisfied with this world, and *cannot* find a home in it. Outward things how vain! when we lean on them merely, and Heaven knows I have striven enough to make my mind its own place. I have resolution for the contest, and will not shrink or faint, but I know not, just at this moment, where to turn . . . .

Experience! why cannot I value thee, and make thee my peculiar household deity, as did our Master, Goethe? I suppose I could, if I had the same reproducing power; but, as it is, Experience only gives me "Byron headache." My mind still leadeth me to new things; I wish to try and try, — and am ashamed too, to be still in this region of experimental philosophy, still afloat. I have thought several times I had grasped "First Principles," but those elegant beings elude me.

LETTERS, 1834

I wish, if possible, to be a Christian and to become so not in sickness and adversity but in health and in the full possession of my reasoning powers — I have felt myself a Christian but it was at times of excitement, skepticism returns besides, a religion should not be adopted from taste but conviction . . . . I have no confidence in God as a Father, if I could believe in Revelation and consequently in an over-ruling Providence many things which seem dark and hateful to me now would be made clear or I could wait — My mind often burns with thoughts on these subjects and I long to pour out my soul to some person of superior calmness and strength and fortunate in more accurate knowledge. I should feel such a quieting reaction. But generally I think it is best I should go through these conflicts alone. The process will be slower, more irksome, more distressing, but the result will be all my own and I shall feel greater confidence in it.

LETTERS, 1835

On the subject of Christianity, my mind is clear. If Divine, it will stand the test of any comparison. I believe the reason it has so imperfectly answered to the aspirations of its Founder is, that men have received it on external grounds. I believe that a religion, thus received, may give the life an external decorum, but will never open the fountains of holiness in the soul.

LETTERS, 1840

There is one only guide, the voice in the heart that asks — Was thy wish sincere? If so thou canst not stray from nature, nor be so perverted but she will make thee true again. I must take my own path, and learn from them all, without being paralyzed for to day. We need great energy, and self-reliance to endure to day. My age may not be the best, my position may be bad, my character ill formed, but thou, Oh Spirit, hast no regard to aught but the seeking heart, and if I try to walk upright will [thou] guide me? What despair must he feel who after a whole life passed in trying to build up himself, resolves that it would have been far better, if he had kept still as the clod of the valley, or yielded easily as the leaf to every breeze. A path has been appointed me. I have walked in it as steadily as I could. "I am what I am." That which I am not, teach me in the others. I will bear the pain of imperfection, but not of doubt.

JOURNAL, 1842

21

For myself, I believe in Christ because I can do without him; because the truth he announces I see elsewhere intimated; because it is fore-shadowed in the very nature of my own being. But I do not wish to do without him. He is constantly aiding and answering me. Only I will not lay any undue and exclusive emphasis on him. When he comes to me I will receive him; when I feel inclined to go by myself, I will. I do not reject the church either. Let men who can with sincerity live in it. I would not — for I believe far more widely than any body of men I know. And as nowhere I worship less than in the places set apart for that purpose, I will not seem to do so. The blue sky seen above the opposite roof preaches better than any brother, because, at present, a freer, simpler medium of religion. When great souls arise again that dare to be entirely free, yet are humble, gentle, and patient, I will listen, if they wish to speak. But that time is not nigh; these I see around me, here and in Europe, are mostly weak and young.

A CREDO

What is done here at home in my heart is my religion. I said to H[edge] I see not one step before me, and my only act is to live to day, and not hasten to conclusions. Let others choose their way, I feel that mine is to keep my equipoise as steadfastly as I may, to see, to think, a faithful skeptic, to reject nothing but accept nothing till it is affirmed in the due order of mine own nature. I belong nowhere. I have pledged myself to nothing. God and the soul and nature are all my creed, subdivisions are unimportant. — As to your Church, I do not deny the church, who can that holds communion on themes of permanent interest as I do with several minds. I have my church where I am by turns priest and lay man. I take these simpler modes, if the world prefers more complex, let it. I act for myself, but prescribe for none other.

JOURNAL, 1842

The Indian is steady to that simple creed, which forms the basis of all this mythology; that there is a God, and a life beyond this; a right and wrong which each man can see, betwixt which each man should choose; that good brings with it its reward and vice its punishment.

Their moral code, if not refined as that of civilized nations, is clear and noble in the stress laid upon truth and fidelity. And all unprejudiced observers bear testimony that the Indians, until broken from their old anchorage by intercourse with the whites, who offer them, instead, a religion of which they furnish neither interpretation nor example, were singularly virtuous, if virtue be allowed to consist in a man's acting up to his own ideas of right.

SUMMER ON THE LAKES

The God Brahma, while on earth, was set to fill up a valley, but he had only a basket given him in which to fetch earth for this purpose; so is it with us all. No leaps, no starts will avail us, by patient crystallization alone the equal temper of wisdom is attainable. Sit at home and the spirit-world will look in at your window with moonlit eyes; run out to find it, and rainbow and golden cup will have vanished and left you the beggarly child you were. The better part of wisdom is a sublime prudence, a pure and patient truth that will receive nothing it is not sure it can permanently lay to heart.

SUMMER ON THE LAKES

I remain fixed to be without churlishness or coldness as much alone as possible. It is best for me — I am not fitted to be loved and it pains me to have close dealings with those who do not love, to whom my feelings are "strange." Kindness and esteem are very well, I am willing to receive and bestow them, but these, alone are not worth feelings such as mine, and I wish I may make no more mistakes, but keep chaste for mine own people. I have got beyond what gave me so much pain in the month of May, but it will never seem right, I fear. Looking today on the Miniature occasioned me painful retrospections. There is no hour of absolute beauty in all my past though some have been made musical by heavenly hope, many, dignified by intelligence.

JOURNAL, 1844

But if you ask me what offices they may fill; I reply — any. I do not care what case you put; let them be sea-captains, if you will. I do not doubt there are women well fitted for such an office, and, if so, I should be glad to see them in it . . . .

I think women need, especially at this juncture, a much greater range of occupation than they have, to rouse their latent powers. A party of travellers lately visited a lonely hut on a mountain. There they found an old woman that told them she and her husband had lived there forty years. "Why," they said, "did you choose so barren a spot?" She "did not know; *it was the man's notion.*"

WOMAN IN THE NINETEENTH CENTURY

As to this living so entirely for men, I should think when it was proposed to women they would feel, at least, some spark of the old spirit of races allied to our own. If he is to be my bridegroom and lord, cries Brunhilda, he must first be able to pass through fire and water. I will serve at the banquet, says the Walkyrie, but only him who, in the trial of deadly combat, has shown himself a hero.

If women are to be bond-maids, let it be to men superior to women in fortitude, in aspiration, in moral power, in refined sense of beauty! You who give yourselves "to be supported," or because "one must love something," are they who make the lot of the sex such that mothers are sad when daughters are born.

WOMAN IN THE NINETEENTH CENTURY

Proclus teaches that every life has, in its sphere, a totality or wholeness of the animating powers of the other spheres; having only, as its own characteristic, a predominance of some one power . . . . In the sphere of Jupiter, energy is predominant — with Venus, beauty; but each comprehends and apprehends all the others.

When the same community of life and consciousness of mind begins among men, humanity will have, positively and finally, subjugated its brute elements and Titanic childhood; criticism will have perished; arbitrary limits and ignorant censure be impossible; all will have entered upon the liberty of law, and the harmony of common growth.

Then Apollo will sing to his lyre what Vulcan forges on the anvil, and the Muse weave anew the tapestries of Minerva.

It is, therefore, only in the present crisis that the preference is given to Minerva. The power of continence must establish the legitimacy of freedom, the power of self-poise the perfection of motion.

Every relation, every gradation of nature is incalculably precious, but only to the soul which is poised upon itself, and to whom no loss, no change, can bring dull discord, for it is in harmony with the central soul.

WOMAN IN THE NINETEENTH CENTURY

"Is it not enough," cries the irritated trader, "that you have done all you could to break up the national union, and thus destroy the prosperity of our country, but now you must be trying to break up family union, to take my wife away from the cradle and the kitchen hearth to vote at polls, and preach from a pulpit? Of course, if she does such things, she cannot attend to those of her own sphere. She is happy enough as she is. She has more leisure than I have, every means of improvement, every indulgence."

"Have you asked her whether she was satisfied with these *indulgences?*"

"No, but I know she is. She is too amiable to wish what would make me unhappy, and too judicious to wish to step beyond the sphere of her sex. I will never consent to have our peace disturbed by any such discussions."

"'Consent — you?' it is not consent from you that is in question, it is assent from your wife."

"Am not I the head of my house?"

"You are not the head of your wife. God has given her a mind of her own."

WOMAN IN THE NINETEENTH CENTURY

The position I early was enabled to take was one of self-reliance. And were all women as sure of their wants as I was, the result would be the same. But they are so overloaded with precepts by guardians, who think that nothing is so much to be dreaded for a woman as originality of thought or character, that their minds are impeded by doubts till they lose their chance of fair, free proportions. The difficulty is to get them to the point from which they shall naturally develop self-respect, and learn self-help.

Once I thought that men would help to forward this state of things more than I do now. I saw so many of them wretched in the connections they had formed in weakness and vanity. They seemed so glad to esteem women whenever they could.

WOMAN IN THE NINETEENTH CENTURY

I have no doubt, however, that a large proportion of women would give themselves to the same employments as now, because there are circumstances that must lead them. Mothers will delight to make the nest soft and warm. Nature would take care of that; no need to clip the wings of any bird that wants to soar and sing, or finds in itself the strength of pinion for a migratory flight unusual to its kind. The difference would be that *all* need not be constrained to employments, for which *some* are unfit.

I have urged upon the sex self-subsistence in its two forms of self-reliance and self-impulse, because I believe them to be the needed means of the present juncture.

I have urged on woman independence of man, not that I do not think the sexes mutually needed by one another, but because in woman this fact has led to an excessive devotion, which has cooled love, degraded marriage, and prevented either sex from being what it should be to itself or the other.

I wish woman to live, *first* for God's sake. Then she will not make an imperfect man her god, and thus sink to idolatry. Then she will not take what is not fit for her from a sense of weakness and poverty. Then, if she finds what she needs in man embodied, she will know how to love, and be worthy of being loved.

By being more a soul, she will not be less woman, for nature is perfected through spirit.

Now there is no woman, only an overgrown child.

WOMAN IN THE NINETEENTH CENTURY

Once two fine figures stood before me, thus. The father of very intellectual aspect, his falcon eye softened by affection as he looked down on his fair child, she the image of himself, only more graceful and brilliant in expression. I was reminded of Southey's Kehama; when lo, the dream was rudely broken. They were talking of education, and he said,

"I shall not have Maria brought too forward. If she knows too much, she will never find a husband; superior women hardly ever can."

"Surely," said his wife, with a blush, "you wish Maria to be as good and wise as she can, whether it will help her to marriage or not."

"No," he persisted, "I want her to have a sphere and a home, and some one to protect her when I am gone."

It was a trifling incident, but made a deep impression. I felt that the holiest relations fail to instruct the unprepared and perverted mind. If this man, indeed, could have looked at it on the other side, he was the last that would have been willing to have been taken himself for the home and protection he could give, but would have been much more likely to repeat the tale of Alcibiades with his phials.

But men do *not* look at both sides, and women must leave off asking them and being influenced by them, but retire within themselves, and explore the groundwork of life till they find their peculiar secret. Then, when they come forth again, renovated and baptized, they will know how to turn all dross to gold, and will be rich and free though they live in a hut, tranquil, if in a crowd. Then their sweet singing shall not be from passionate impulse, but the lyrical overflow of a divine rapture, and a new music shall be evolved from this many-chorded world.

Grant her, then, for a while, the armor and the javelin. Let her put from her the press of other minds and meditate in virgin loneliness. The same idea shall re-appear in due time as Muse, or Ceres, the all-kindly patient Earth-Spirit.

WOMAN IN THE NINETEENTH CENTURY

What I mean by the Muse is the unimpeded clearness of the intuitive powers which a perfectly truthful adherence to every admonition of the higher instincts would bring to a finely organized human being. It may appear as prophecy or as poesy. It enabled Cassandra to foresee the results of actions passing round her; the Seeress to behold the true character of the person through the mask of his customary life. (Sometimes she saw a feminine form behind the man, sometimes the reverse.) It enabled the daughter of Linnaeus to see the soul of the flower exhaling from the flower . . . . Sight must be verified by life before it can deserve the honors of piety and genius. Yet sight comes first, and of this sight of the world of causes, this approximation to the region of primitive motions, women I hold to be especially capable. Even without equal freedom with the other sex, they have already shown themselves so, and should these faculties have free play, I believe they will open new, deeper and purer sources of joyous inspiration than have as yet refreshed the earth.

WOMAN IN THE NINETEENTH CENTURY

If any individual live too much in relations, so that he becomes a stranger to the resources of his own nature, he falls, after a while, into a distraction, or imbecility, from which he can only be cured by a time of isolation, which gives the renovating fountains time to rise up. With a society it is the same. Many minds, deprived of the traditionary or instinctive means of passing a cheerful existence, must find help in self-impulse, or perish. It is therefore that, while any elevation, in the view of union, is to be hailed with joy, we shall not decline celibacy as the great fact of the time. It is one from which no vow, no arrangement, can at present save a thinking mind. For now the rowers are pausing on their oars; they wait a change before they can pull together. All tends to illustrate the thought of a wise cotemporary. Union is only possible to those who are units. To be fit for relations in time, souls, whether of man or woman, must be able to do without them in the spirit.

It is therefore that I would have woman lay aside all thought, such as she habitually cherishes, of being taught and led by men. I would have her, like the Indian girl, dedicate herself to the Sun, the Sun of Truth, and go no where if his beams did not make clear the path. I would have her free from compromise, from complaisance, from help-lessness, because I would have her good enough and strong enough to love one and all beings, from the fulness, not the poverty of being.

Men, as at present instructed, will not help this work, because they also are under the slavery of habit.

WOMAN IN THE NINETEENTH CENTURY

What others can do, — whether all that has been said is the mere restlessness of discontent, or there are thoughts really struggling for utterance, — will be tested now. A perfectly free organ is to be offered for the expression of individual thought and character. There are no party measures to be carried, no particular standard to be set up. A fair, calm tone, a recognition of universal principles, will, I hope, pervade the essays in every form. I trust there will be a spirit neither of dogmatism nor of compromise, and that this journal [The *Dial*] will aim, not at leading public opinion, but at stimulating each man to judge for himself, and to think more deeply and more nobly, by letting him see how some minds are kept alive by a wise self-trust. We must not be sanguine as to the amount of talent which will be brought to bear on this publication. All concerned are rather indifferent, and there is no great promise for the present. We cannot show high culture, and I doubt about vigorous thought. But we shall manifest free action as far as it goes, and a high aim. It were much if a periodical could be kept open, not to accomplish any outward object, but merely to afford an avenue for what of liberal and calm thought might be originated among us, by the wants of individual minds.

MEMOIRS

From a very early age I have felt that I was not born to the common womanly lot. I knew I should never find a being who could keep the key of my character; that there would be none on whom I could always lean, from whom I could always learn; that I should be a pilgrim and sojourner on earth, and that the birds and foxes would be surer of a place to lay the head than I. You understand me, of course; such beings can only find their homes in hearts. All material luxuries, all arrangements of society, are mere conveniences to them.

This thought, all whose bearings I did not, indeed, understand, affected me sometimes with sadness, sometimes with pride. I mourned that I never should have a thorough experience of life, never know the full riches of my being; I was proud that I was to test myself in the sternest way, that I was always to return to myself, to be my own priest, pupil, parent, child, husband, and wife. All this I did not understand as I do now; but this destiny of the thinker, and (shall I dare to say it?) of the poetic priestess, sibylline, dwelling in the cave, or amid the Lybian sands, lay yet enfolded in my mind. Accordingly, I did not look on any of the persons, brought into relation with me, with common womanly eyes.

Yet, as my character is, after all, still more feminine than masculine, it would sometimes happen that I put more emotion into a state than I myself knew. I really was capable of attachment, though it never seemed so till the hour of separation. And if a connexion was torn up by the roots, the soil of my existence showed an unsightly wound, which long refused to clothe itself in verdure.

MEMOIRS

In early years, when, though so frank as to the thoughts of the mind, I put no heart confidence in any human being, my refuge was in my journal. I have burned those records of my youth, with its bitter tears, and struggles, and aspirations. Those aspirations were high, and have gained only broader foundations and wider reach. But the leaves had done their work. For years to write there, instead of speaking, had enabled me to soothe myself; and the Spirit was often my friend, when I sought no other.

MEMOIRS

It is true that I have had less outward aid, in after years, than most women, but that is of little consequence. Religion was early awakened in my soul, a sense that what the soul is capable to ask it must attain, and that, though I might be aided and instructed by others, I must depend on myself as the only constant friend. This self-dependence, which was honored in me, is deprecated as a fault in most women. They are taught to learn their rule from without, not to unfold it from within.

WOMAN IN THE NINETEENTH CENTURY

There are two aspects of woman's nature, represented by the ancients as Muse and Minerva . . . .

If it has been the tendency of these remarks to call woman rather to the Minerva side, — if I, unlike the more generous writer, have spoken from society no less than the soul, — let it be pardoned! It is love that has caused this, love for many incarcerated souls, that might be freed, could the idea of religious self-dependence be established in them, could the weakening habit of dependence on others be broken up.

WOMAN IN THE NINETEENTH CENTURY

Truth is the nursing mother of genius. No man can be absolutely true to himself, eschewing cant, compromise, servile imitation, and complaisance, without becoming original, for there is in every creature a fountain of life which, if not choked back by stones and other dead rubbish, will create a fresh atmosphere, and bring to life fresh beauty. And it is the same with the nation as with the individual man.

The best work we do for the future is by such truth. By use of that, in whatever way, we harrow the soil and lay it open to the sun and air. The winds from all quarters of the globe bring seed enough, and there is nothing wanting but preparation of the soil, and freedom in the atmosphere, for ripening of a new and golden harvest.

AMERICAN LITERATURE

In the chamber of death, I prayed in very early years, "Give me truth; cheat me by no illusion." O, the granting of this prayer is sometimes terrible to me! I walk over the burning ploughshares, and they sear my feet. Yet nothing but truth will do; no love will serve that is not eternal, and as large as the universe; no philanthropy in executing whose behests I myself become unhealthy; no creative genius which bursts asunder my life, to leave it a poor black chrysalid behind. And yet this last is too true of me.

MEMOIRS

The church was the growth of human nature, and it is so still. It is but one result of the impulse which makes two friends clasp one another's hands, look into one another's eyes at sight of beauty, or the utterance of a feeling of piety. So soon as the Spirit has mourned and sought, and waited long enough to open new depths, and has found something to express, there will again be a Cultus, a Church. The very people who say that none is needed, make one at once. They talk with, they write to one another. They listen to music, they sustain themselves with the poets; they like that one voice should tell the thoughts of several minds, one gesture proclaim that the same life is at the same moment in many breasts.

I am myself most happy in my lonely Sundays, and do not feel the need of any social worship, as I have not for several years, which I have passed in the same way. Sunday is to me priceless as a day of peace and solitary reflection . . . . After much troubling of the waters of my life, a radiant thought of the meaning and beauty of earthly existence will descend like a healing angel. The stillness permits me to hear a pure tone from the One in All. But often I am not alone. The many now, whose hearts, panting for truth and love, have been made known to me, whose lives flow in the same direction as mine, and are enlightened by the same star, are with me. I am in church, the church invisible, undefiled by inadequate expression. Our communion is perfect; it is that of a common aspiration; and where two or three are gathered together in one region, whether in the flesh or the spirit, He will grant their request. Other communion would be a happiness, — to break together the bread of mutual thought, to drink the wine of loving life, — but it is not necessary.

LETTERS, N.D.

The Majesty of Earth

Margaret Fuller did not deny the tragic element in human existence. She had experienced too much pain in her own life to be a faithful idealist. Rather, she embraced the sublime in life and nature — the "titanic" as well as the beautiful. For Fuller, it was essential to be guided by our "own particular star" in navigating the rapids of life. Thus we can experience the pulse and excitement of existence while at the same time keeping a sense of balance and perspective. Nature itself teaches this truth, as she learned from the falls at Niagara, the prairies of the American Midwest, and a lonely mountaintop in Scotland.

The mere Idealist vexes me more than the mere Realist, because he seems to me never to have lived. He might as well have been a butterfly; he does not know the human element.

I love the stern Titanic part, I love the crag, even the Drachenfels of life — I love its roaring sea that dashes against the crag — I love its sounding cataract, its lava rush, its whirlwind, its rivers generating the lotus and the crocodile, its hot sands with their white bones, patient camels, and majestic columns toppling to the sky in all the might of-dust. I love its dens and silvery gleaming caverns, its gnomes, its serpents, and the tiger's sudden spring. Nay! I would not be without what I know better, its ghostly northern firs, haggard with ice, its solitary tarns, tearful eyes of the lone forest, its trembling lizards and its wounded snakes dragging to secretest recesses their slow length along.

Who can know these and, other myriad other children of Chaos and old night, who can know the awe the horror and the majesty of earth, yet be content with the blue sky alone. Not I for one. I love the love lit dome above. I cannot live without mine own particular star; but my foot is on the earth and I wish to walk over it until my wings be grown. I will use my microscope as well as my telescope. And oh ye flowers, ye fruits, and, nearer kindred yet, stones with your veins so worn by fire and water, and here and there disclosing streaks of golden ore, let us know one another before we part. Tell me your secret, tell me mine. To be human is also something?

LETTERS, 1839

When I feel, as I do this morning, the poem of existence, I am repaid for all trial. The bitterness of wounded affection, the disgust at unworthy care, the aching sense of how far deeds are transcended by our lowest aspirations, pass away as I lean on the bosom of Nature, and inhale new life from her breath.

MEMOIRS

Our house, though comfortable, was very ugly, and in a neighborhood which I detested, — every dwelling and its appurtenances having a *mesquin* and huddled look. I liked nothing about us except the tall graceful elms before the house, and the dear little garden behind. Our back door opened on a high flight of steps, by which I went down to a green plot, much injured in my ambitious eyes by the presence of the pump and the tool-house. This opened into a little garden, full of choice flowers and fruit-trees, which was my mother's delight, and was carefully kept. Here I felt at home. A gate opened thence into the fields, — a wooden gate made of boards, in a high, unpainted board wall, and embowered in the clematis creeper. This gate I used to open to see the sunset heaven; beyond this black frame I did not step, for I liked to look at the deep gold behind it. How exquisitely happy I was in its beauty, and how I loved the silvery wreaths of my protecting vine!

AUTOBIOGRAPHICAL ROMANCE

In the evening I took a walk with W[aldo]. Looking at the moon in the river he said the same thing as in his letter, how each twinkling light breaking there summons to demand the whole secret, and how "promising, promising nature never fulfills what she thus gives us a right to expect." I said I never could meet him here, the beauty does not stimulate me to ask *why?* and press to the centre, I was satisfied for the moment, full as if my existence was filled out, for nature had said the very word that was lying in my heart. Then we had an excellent talk: We agreed that my god was Love, his Truth. W. said that these statements alternate, of course, in every mind, the only difference was in which you were most at home, that he liked the pure mathematics of the thing.

JOURNAL, 1842

The great drawback upon the lives of these settlers, at present, is the unfitness of the women for their new lot. It has generally been the choice of the men, and the women follow, as women will, doing their best for affection's sake, but too often in heart- sickness and weariness. Beside it frequently not being a choice or conviction of their own minds that it is best to be here, their part is the hardest, and they are least fitted for it. The men can find assistance in field labor, and recreation with the gun and fishing-rod. Their bodily strength is greater, and enables them to bear and enjoy both these forms of life . . . .

With all these disadvantages for work, their resources for pleasure are fewer. When they can leave the housework, they have not learnt to ride, to drive, to row, alone. Their culture has too generally been that given to women to make them "the ornaments of society." They can dance, but not draw; talk French, but know nothing of the language of flowers; neither in childhood were allowed to cultivate them, lest they should tan their complexions. Accustomed to the pavement of Broadway, they dare not tread the wildwood paths for fear of rattlesnakes!

Seeing much of this joylessness, and inaptitude, both of body and mind, for a lot which would be full of blessings for those prepared for it, we could not but look with deep interest on the little girls, and hope they would grow up with the strength of body, dexterity, simple tastes, and resources that would fit them to enjoy and refine the western farmer's life.

SUMMER ON THE LAKES

Although I have little to tell, I feel that I have learnt a great deal of the Indians, from observing them even in this broken and degraded condition. There is a language of eye and motion which cannot be put into words, and which teaches what words never can. I feel acquainted with the soul of this race; I read its nobler thought in their defaced figures. There *was* a greatness, unique and precious, which he who does not feel will never duly appreciate the majesty of nature in this American continent.

I have mentioned that the Indian orator, who addressed the agents on this occasion, said, the difference between the white man and the red man is this: "the white man no sooner came here, than he thought of preparing the way for his posterity; the red man never thought of this."

SUMMER ON THE LAKES

At Inversnaid, we took a boat to go down Loch Lomond, to the little inn of Rowardennan, from which the ascent is made of Ben Lomond . . . . On reaching the peak, the sight was one of beauty and grandeur such as imagination never painted. You see around you no plain ground, but on every side constellations, or groups of hills, exquisitely dressed in the soft purple of the heather, amid which gleam the lakes, like eyes that tell the secrets of the earth, and drink in those of the heavens. Peak beyond peak caught from the shifting light all the colors of the prism, and, on the furthest, angel companies seemed hovering in glorious white robes.

About four o'clock we began our descent. Near the summit, the traces of the path are not distinct, and I said to Mr. S., after a while, that we had lost it. He said he thought that was of no consequence; we could find our way down. I said I thought it was, as the ground was full of springs that were bridged over in the path way. He accordingly went to look for it, and I stood still, because I was so tired I did not like to waste any labor.

Soon he called to me that he had found it, and I followed in the direction where he seemed to be. But I mistook, overshot it, and saw him no more . . . .

I then attempted to descend in the water-course, but, finding that impracticable, climbed on the hill again, and let myself down by the heather, for it was very steep, and full of deep holes. With great fatigue, I got to the bottom, but when I was about to cross the water-course there, I felt afraid, it looked so deep in the dim twilight. I got down as far as I could by the root of a tree, and threw down a stone. It sounded very hollow, and I was afraid to jump. The shepherds told me afterwards, if I had, I should probably have killed myself, it was so deep, and the bed of the torrent full of sharp stones.

I then tried to ascend the hill again, for there was no other way to get off it; but soon sank down utterly exhausted. When able to get up again, and look about me, it was completely dark. I saw, far below me, a light, that looked about as big as a pin's head, that I knew to be from the inn at Rowardennan, but heard no sound except the rush of the waterfall, and the sighing of the night wind.

For the first few minutes after I perceived I had come to my night's lodging, such as it was, the circumstance looked appalling. I was very lightly clad, my feet and dress were very wet, I had only a little shawl to throw round me, and the cold autumn wind had already come, and the night mist was to fall on me, all fevered and exhausted as I was. I thought I should not live through the night, or, if I did, I must be an invalid henceforward . . . .

It was sublime indeed, — a never-to-be-forgotten presentation of stern, serene realities. At last came the signs of day, — the gradual clearing and breaking up; some faint sounds from I know not what; the little flies, too, arose from their bed amid the purple heather, and bit me. Truly they were very welcome to do so. But what was my disappointment to find the mist so thick, that I could see neither lake nor inn, nor anything to guide me. I had to go by guess . . . . I kept on scrambling, as it happened, in the right direction, till, about seven, some of the shepherds found me. The moment they came, all my feverish strength departed, and they carried me home, where my arrival relieved my friends of distress far greater than I had undergone; for I had my grand solitude, my Ossianic visions, and the pleasure of sustaining myself; while they had only doubt, amounting to anguish, and a fruitless search through the night.

MEMOIRS

With the first light of dawn I was up and out, and then was glad I had not seen all the night before; it came upon me with such power in its dewy freshness. O! they are beautiful indeed, these rapids! The grace is so much more obvious than the power. I went up through the old Chippeway burying ground to their head, and sat down on a large stone to look. A little way off was one of the home lodges, unlike in shape to the temporary ones at Mackinaw, but these have been described by Mrs. Jameson. Women, too, I saw coming home from the woods, stooping under great loads of cedar boughs, that were strapped upon their backs. But in many European countries women carry great loads, even of wood, upon their backs. I used to hear the girls singing and laughing as they were cutting down boughs at Mackinaw; this part of their employment, though laborious, gives them the pleasure of being a great deal in the free woods.

SUMMER ON THE LAKES

I come to the west prepared for the distaste I must experience at its mushroom growth. I know that where "go ahead" is the only motto, the village cannot grow into the gentle proportions that successive lives, and the gradations of experience involuntarily give. In older countries the house of the son grew from that of the father, as naturally as new joints on a bough. And the cathedral crowned the whole as naturally as the leafy summit the tree. This cannot be here. The march of peaceful is scarce less wanton than that of warlike invasion. The old landmarks are broken down, and the land, for a season, bears none, except of the rudeness of conquest and the needs of the day, whose bivouac fires blacken the sweetest forest glades. I have come prepared to see all this, to dislike it, but not with stupid narrowness to distrust or defame. On the contrary, while I will not be so obliging as to confound ugliness with beauty, discord with harmony, and laud and be contented with all I meet, when it conflicts with my best desires and tastes, I trust by reverent faith to woo the mighty meaning of the scene, perhaps to foresee the law by which a new order, a new poetry is to be evoked from this chaos, and with a curiosity as ardent, but not so selfish as that of Macbeth, to call up the apparitions of future kings from the strange ingredients of the witch's caldron. Thus, I will not grieve that all the noble trees are gone already from this island to feed this caldron, but believe it will have Medea's virtue, and reproduce them in the form of new intellectual growths, since centuries cannot again adorn the land with such.

SUMMER ON THE LAKES

I went out upon the lonely rock which commands so delicious a panoramic view. A very mild breeze had sprung up after the extreme heat. A sunset of the melting kind was succeeded by a perfectly clear moonrise. Here I sat, and thought of Raphael. I was drawn high up in the heaven of beauty, and the mists were dried from the white plumes of contemplation.

Only by emotion do we know thee, Nature. To lean upon thy heart, and feel its pulses vibrate to our own; — that is knowledge, for that is love, the love of infinite beauty, of infinite love. Thought will never make us be born again.

My fault is that I think I feel *too much*. O that my friends would teach me that "simple art of not too much!" How can I expect them to bear the ceaseless eloquence of my nature?

MEMOIRS

As I rode up to the neighborhood of the falls, a solemn awe imperceptibly stole over me, and the deep sound of the ever-hurrying rapids prepared my mind for the lofty emotions to be experienced. When I reached the hotel, I felt a strange indifference about seeing the aspiration of my life's hopes. I lounged about the rooms, read the stage bills upon the walls, looked over the register, and, finding the name of an acquaintance, sent to see if he was still there. What this hesitation arose from, I know not; perhaps it was a feeling of my unworthiness to enter this temple which nature has erected to its God.

At last, slowly and thoughtfully I walked down to the bridge leading to Goat Island, and when I stood upon this frail support, and saw a quarter of a mile of tumbling, rushing rapids, and heard their everlasting roar, my emotions overpowered me, a choking sensation rose to my throat, a thrill rushed through my veins, "my blood ran rippling to my finger's ends." This was the climax of the effect which the falls produced upon me — neither the American nor the British fall moved me as did these rapids. For the magnificence, the sublimity of the latter I was prepared by descriptions and by paintings . . . .

Then arose in my breast a genuine admiration, and a humble adoration of the Being who was the architect of this and of all. Happy were the first discoverers of Niagara, those who could come unawares upon this view and upon that, whose feelings were entirely their own.

SUMMER ON THE LAKES

In Chicago I first saw the beautiful prairie flowers. They were in their glory the first ten days we were there —

The golden and the flame-like flowers.

The flame-like flower I was taught afterwards, by an Indian girl, to call

"Wickapee"; and she told me, too, that its splendors had a useful side, for it was used by the Indians as a remedy for an illness to which they were subject.

Beside these brilliant flowers, which gemmed and gilt the grass in a sunny afternoon's drive near the blue lake, between the low oakwood and the narrow beach, stimulated, whether sensuously by the optic nerve, unused to so much gold and crimson with such tender green, or symbolically through some meaning dimly seen in the flowers, I enjoyed a sort of fairyland exultation never felt before, and the first drive amid the flowers gave me anticipation of the beauty of the prairies.

At first, the prairie seemed to speak of the very desolation of dullness. After sweeping over the vast monotony of the lakes to come to this monotony of land, with all around a limitless horizon, — to walk, and walk, and run, but never climb, oh! it was too dreary for any but a Hollander to bear. How the eye greeted the approach of a sail, or the smoke of a steamboat; it seemed that any thing so animated must come from a better land, where mountains gave religion to the scene . . . .

But after I had rode out, and seen the flowers and seen the sun set with that calmness seen only in the prairies, and the cattle winding slowly home to their homes in the "island groves" — peacefullest of sights — I began to love because I began to know the scene, and shrank no longer from "the encircling vastness."

It is always thus with the new form of life; we must learn to look at it by its own standard. At first, no doubt my accustomed eye kept saying, if the mind did not, What! no distant mountains? what, no valleys? But after a while I would ascend the roof of the house where we lived, and pass many hours, needing no sight but the moon reigning in the heavens, or starlight falling upon the lake, till all the lights were out in the island grove of men beneath my feet, and felt nearer heaven that there was nothing but this lovely, still reception on the earth; no towering mountains, no deep tree-shadows, nothing but plain earth and water bathed in light.

SUMMER ON THE LAKES

No heaven need wear a lovelier aspect than earth did this afternoon, after the clearing up of the shower. We traversed the blooming plain, unmarked by any road, only the friendly track of wheels which tracked, not broke the grass. Our stations were not from town to town, but from grove to grove. These groves first floated like blue islands in the distance. As we drew nearer, they seemed fair parks, and the little log houses on the edge, with their curling smokes, harmonized beautifully with them.

One of these groves, Ross's grove, we reached just at sunset. It was of the noblest trees I saw during this journey, for the trees generally were not large or lofty, but only of fair proportions. Here they were large enough to form with their clear stems pillars for grand cathedral aisles. There was space enough for crimson light to stream through upon the floor of water which the shower had left. As we slowly plashed through, I thought I was never in a better place for vespers.

SUMMER ON THE LAKES

Not far from the river was a high crag, called the Pine Rock, which looks out, as our guide observed, like a helmet above the brow of the country. It seems as if the water left here and there a vestige of forms and materials that preceded its course, just to set off its new and richer designs.

The aspect of this country was to me enchanting, beyond any I have ever seen, from its fullness of expression, its bold and impassioned sweetness. Here the flood of emotion has passed over and marked everywhere its course by a smile. The fragments of rock touch it with a wildness and liberality which give just the needed relief. I should never be tired here, though I have elsewhere seen country of more secret and alluring charms, better calculated to stimulate and suggest. Here the eye and heart are filled.

How happy the Indians must have been here! It is not long since they were driven away, and the ground, above and below, is full of their traces.

SUMMER ON THE LAKES

A God, a Beauty and Perfection

Margaret Fuller was subject to visions of a mystical nature and believed that religion should be grounded in intuition and ecstasy. Her visions were of an "Eternal Progression," a great chain of being — "uncontainable and uncontained" — rising to consciousness through the material and animal worlds, and coming to awareness in humanity. Fuller believed that great religious teachers like Jesus called on humanity to manifest the divine spirit in life. Rather than venerating such teachers, Fuller sought to emulate them with her own prophetic vision of a more perfect world.

Loving or feeble natures need a positive religion, a visible refuge, a protection, as much in the passionate season of youth as in those stages nearer to the grave. But mine is not such. My pride is superior to any feelings I have yet experienced: my affection is strong admiration, not the necessity of giving or receiving assistance or sympathy. When disappointed, I do not ask or wish consolation, — I wish to know and feel my pain, to investigate its nature and its source; I will not have my thoughts diverted, or my feelings soothed; 'tis therefore that my young life is so singularly barren of illusions. I know, I feel the time must come when this proud and impatient heart shall be stilled, and turn from the ardors of Search and Action, to lean on something above. But — shall I say it? — the thought of that calmer era is to me a thought of deepest sadness; so remote from my present being is that future existence, which still the mind may conceive. I believe in Eternal Progression. I believe in a God, a Beauty and Perfection to which I am to strive all my life for assimilation. From these two articles of belief, I draw the rules by which I strive to regulate my life. But, though I reverence all religions as necessary to the happiness of man, I am yet ignorant of the religion of Revelation. Tangible promises! well defined hopes! are the things of which I do not *now* feel the need. At present my soul is intent on this life, and I think of religion as its rule; and, in my opinion, this is the natural and proper course from youth to age.

LETTERS, 1829

One day lives always in my memory; one chastest, heavenliest day of communion with the soul of things. It was Thanksgiving-Day. I was free to be alone; in the meditative woods, by the choked-up fountain I passed its hours, each of which contained ages of thought and emotion. I saw then how idle were my griefs; that I had acquired *the thought* of each object which had been taken from me, that more extended personal relations would only have given me pleasures which then seemed not worth my care, and which would surely have dimmed my sense of the spiritual meaning of all which had passed. I felt how true it was that nothing in any being which was fit for me, could long be kept from me, and that if separation could be, real intimacy had never been. All the films seemed to drop from my existence, and I was sure that I should never starve in this desert world, but that manna would drop from heaven, if I would but rise with every rising sun to gather it.

In the evening I went into the church-yard; the moon sailed above the rosy clouds. That cresent moon rose above the heavenward-pointing spire. At that hour a vision came upon my soul, whose final scene last month interpreted. The rosy clouds of illusion are all vanished, the moon has waxed to full. May my life be a church, full of devout thoughts, and solemn music. I pray thus, my dearest child: "Our Father, let not the heaviest shower be spared, let not the gardener forbear his knife, till the fair hopeful tree of existence be brought to its fullest blossom and fruit!"

LETTERS, 1838

Why should not I have a vision? — O I have been so happy — have done and felt every-thing with such enjoyment — It was really Sabbath — I felt so very right when I was going to and from church and so prayerfull in it. The day has been divine as if nature wished to make up for her late coldness by crowding all June into one day. Such gorgeous light, such rich deep shadows — such sweet, *sweet* west wind! And this evening I have been sitting in the piazza hearing it rustle the vines against the Moon's benignant face and thinking through Alroy which I have been reading — I lived it all through and set it to musick in my soul. This is an era — I have never been happy on a moonlight evening (I mean in a constant happy mood — I always have high flights and keen flashes) except in two instances and those were rapture — but this is such a sweet and strange composure. I never felt any-thing like it except on Thanksgiving day which you may remember I told you about. But that was far better — I shall never know a day like that again — it was like the mansions of the blest. Today I am wide awake and notice every-thing — I am quite well today and can let Heaven's free wind blow upon me without being shudderingly reminded that I am framed of "suffering clay."

LETTERS, 1833

I have let myself be cheated out of my Sunday, by going to hear Mr. [Dewey]. As he began by reading the first chapter of Isaiah, and the fourth of John's Epistle, I made mental comments with pure delight . . . . But straightway uprose the preacher to deny mysteries, to deny the second birth, to deny influx, and to renounce the sovereign gift of insight, for the sake of what he deemed a "*rational*" exercise of will. As he spoke I could not choose but deny him all through, and could scarce refrain from rising to expound, in the light of my own faith, the words of those wiser Jews which had been read. Was it not a sin to exchange friendly greeting as we parted, and yet tell him no word of what was in my mind?

Still I saw why he looked at things as he did. The old religionists did talk about "grace, conversion," and the like, technically, without striving to enter into the idea, till they quite lost sight of it. Undervaluing the intellect, they became slaves of a sect, instead of organs of the Spirit.

45

This Unitarianism has had its place. There was a time for asserting "the dignity of human nature," and for explaining total depravity into temporary inadequacy, a time to say that the truths of Essence, if simplified at all in statement from their infinite variety of existence, should be spoken of as One rather than Three . . . . [Y]et the time seems now to have come for reinterpreting the old dogmas. I would now preach the Holy Ghost as zealously as they have been preaching Man, and faith instead of the understanding and mysticism instead, &c.

LETTERS, 1840

I do not mean to lay an undue stress upon the position and office of man, merely because I am of his race, and understand best the scope of his destiny. The history of the earth, the motions of the heavenly bodies suggest already modes of being higher than his, and which fulfilll more deeply this office of interpretation. But I do suppose his life to be the rivet in one series of links in the great chain, and that all these higher existences are analogous to his. Music suggests them, and when carried on these strong wings through realms which on the ground we discern but dimly, we foresee how the next step in the soul's upward course shall interpret man to the universe as he now interprets those forms beneath himself; for there is ever evolving a consciousness of consciousness, and a soul of the soul. To know is to bring to light somewhat yet to be known. And as we elucidate the previous workings of spirit, we ourselves become a new material for its development.

A CREDO

Wherever man remains imbedded in nature, whether from sensuality or because he is not yet awakened to consciousness, the purpose of the whole remains unfulfillled, hence our displeasure when man is not in a sense *above* nature. Yet when he is not bound so closely with all other manifestations, as duly to express their spirit, we are also displeased. He must be at once the highest form of nature and conscious of the meaning she has been striving successively to unfold through those below him.

Centuries pass, — whole races of men are expended in the effort to produce one that shall realize this idea and publish spirit in the human form. But here and there there is a degree of success. Life enough is lived through a man to justify the great difficulties and obstructions attendant on the existence of mankind.

A CREDO

We understand, though we cannot explain the mystery of something gained where all already is.

God, we say, is Love. If we believe this we must trust Him. Whatever has been permitted by the law of being must be *for* good, and only *in time not good*. We do trust Him and are led forward by experience. Sight gives experience of outward life, faith of inward. We then discern, however faintly, the necessary harmony of the two lives. The moment we have broken through an obstruction, not accidentally, but by the aid of faith, we begin to realize why any was permitted. We begin to interpret the universe and deeper depths are opened with each soul that is convinced. For it would seem that the Divine expressed His meaning to Himself more distinctly in man than in the other forms of our sphere, and through him uttered distinctly the Hallelujah which the other forms of nature only intimate.

A CREDO

The spirit ascends through every form of nature into man, and no doubt here should make the complete animal instinctive man before unfolding his higher nature. But it was no accident that the serpent entered Eden, that the regular order of things was destroyed, that a painful throe accompanies every precious truth. When the soul has mastered it all, when it has learnt the secret in all its series, then there shall be no more breaks, no sluggishness, no premature fruit, but every thought be unfolded in its due order. Till then let us stand where our feet are placed and learn bit by bit, secure that it must be the destiny of each man to fill the whole circle.

JOURNAL, 1842

There is a spirit uncontainable and uncontained. — Within it all manifestation is contained, whether of good (accomplishment) or evil (obstruction). To itself its depths are unknown. By living it seeks to know itself, thus evolving plants, animals, men, suns, stars, angels, and, it is to be presumed an infinity of forms not yet visible in the horizon of this being who now writes.

A CREDO

Man is himself one tree in the garden of the spirit. From his trunk grow many branches, social contracts, art, literature, religion, etc. The trunk gives the history of the human race. It has grown up higher into the heavens, but its several acorns, though each expressed the all, did not ripen beyond certain contours and a certain size.

In the history of matter, however, laws have been more and more clearly discerned, and so in the history of spirit, many features of the *God-man* have put forth; several limbs, disengaged themselves. One is what men call revelation, different from other kinds only in being made through the acts and words of men. Its law is identical whether displaying itself as genius or piety, but its modes of expression are distinct dialects though of similar structure.

The way it is done is this. As the Oak desires to plant its acorns, so do souls become the fathers of souls. Some do this through the body, others through the intellect. The first class are citizens; the second artists, philosophers, lawgivers, poets, saints, — All these are anointed, all Immanuel, all Messiah, so far as they are true to the law of their incorruptible existence; brutes and devils so far as they are subjected to that of their corruptible existence.

But yet further, as wherever there is a tendency, a form is gradually evolved as its type; as the rose represents the flower world and is its queen, as the lion and eagle compress within themselves the noblest that is expressed in the animal kingdom, as the telescope and microscope express the high and searching desires of man . . . . It gave laws with Confucius and Moses; it tried them with Brahma, it lived its life of eloquence in the Apollo, it wandered with Osiris. It lived one life as Plato, another as Michael Angelo, or Luther. It has made Gods, it has developed men. Seeking, making it produce ideals of the developments of which humanity is capable, and one of the highest, nay in some respects the very highest it has yet known was the life of Jesus of Nazareth.

A CREDO

I suppose few are so much believers in his history as myself. I believe (*in my own way*) in the long preparation of ages, and the truth of the prophecy. I see a necessity in the character of Jesus why Abraham should be the founder of his nation, Moses its lawgiver, and David its king and poet. I believe in the genesis, as given in the Old Testament. I believe in the prophets, and that they foreknew, not only what their nation required, but what the development of universal man required, a Redeemer, an Atoner, one to make, at the due crisis, voluntarily the sacrifice Abraham would have made of the child of his old age, a lamb of God, taking away the sins of the world. I believe Jesus came when the time was ripe, that he was peculiarly a messenger and son of God. I have nothing to say in denial [of] the story of his birth. Whatever the true circumstances were *in time* he was born of a virgin, and the tale expresses a truth of the soul. I have no objection to the miracles, except where they do not happen to please me. Why should not a soul so consecrate and intent develop new laws and make matter plastic? I can imagine him walking the waves and raising the dead without any violation of my usual habits of thought. He would not remain in the tomb, they say, surely not; death is impossible to such a being. He remained upon earth and all who have met him since *on the way* have felt their souls burn within them. He ascended to Heaven, surely, it could not be otherwise.

But when I say to you, also, that though I think all this really happened, it is of no consequence to me whether it did or not, that the ideal truth such illustrations present to me, is enough, and that if the mind of St. John, for instance, had conceived the whole and offered it to us as a poem, to me, as far as I know, it would be just as real. You see how wide the gulf that separates me from the Christian Church.

A CREDO

Yet you also see that I believe in the history of the Jewish nation and its denouement in Christ, as presenting one great type of spiritual existence. It is very dear to me and occupies a large portion of my thoughts. I have no trouble, so far from the sacrifice required of Abraham, for instance, striking me as it does Mr. Parker, I accept it as prefiguring a thought to be fully expressed by the death of Christ (yet forget not that they who passed their children through the fire to Moloch were pious also, and not more superstitious than an exclusive devotion to Christ has made many of his followers). Do you not place Christ then in a higher place than Socrates, for instance, or Michael Angelo? Yes! Because if his life was not truer, it was deeper, and he is a representative of the ages. But then I consider the Greek Apollo as one also!

A CREDO

I will not loathe sects, persuasions, systems, though I cannot abide in them one moment. I see most men are still in need of them. To them their banners, their tents; let them be Platonists, Fire-worshippers, Christians; let them live in the shadow of the past revelations. But Oh Father of our souls, I seek thee. I seek thee in these forms; and in proportion as they reveal thee more, they lead me beyond themselves. I would learn from them all, looking to thee. I set no limits from the past to my soul or any soul. Countless ages may not produce another worthy to loose the shoes of Jesus of Nazareth; yet there will surely come another manifestation of that *Word* that was in the beginning. For it is not dead, but sleepeth; and if it lives, must declare itself.

All future manifestations will come, like this, — not to destroy the law and the prophets but to fulfill. But as an Abraham called for a Moses, a Moses for a David, so does Christ for another ideal.

We want a life more complete and various than that of Christ. We have had the Messiah to reconcile and teach, let us have another to live out all the symbolical forms of human life with the calm beauty and physical fullness of a Greek god, with the deep consciousness of a Moses, with the holy love and purity of Jesus. Amen!

A CREDO

Do you climb the snowy peaks from whence come the streams, where the atmosphere is rare, where you can see the sky nearer, from which you can get a commanding view of the landscape? I see great disadvantages as well as advantages in this dignified position. I had rather walk myself through all kinds of places, even at the risk of being robbed in the forest, half drowned at the ford, and covered with dust in the street.

I would beat with the living heart of the world, and understand all the moods, even the fancies or fantasies, of nature. I dare to trust to the interpreting spirit to bring me out all right at last — to establish truth through error . . . .

Let me stand in my age with all its waters flowing round me. If they sometimes subdue, they must finally upbear me, for I seek the universal — and that must be the best.

The Spirit, no doubt, leads in every movement of my time: if I seek the How, I shall find it, as well as if I busied myself more with the Why.

Whatever is, is right, if only men are steadily bent to make it so, by comprehending and fulfilling its design.

SUMMER ON THE LAKES

Just so with us at present, we are in the stress of a great stream of change which gives on one side but takes away on the other. Let us keep ready then our light boats, and our bag of seed-grain well protected from the water, that is furniture enough for life at present. We will not sigh for the sacred depths of the slow growing forests, for its secret springs and glades, and wild-flowers. Those are beauteous, but *not ours* and have not this quick springing verdure and these strange wild fowl and fish, and the loud rushing music of the stream enough to tell for one day?

But let us be wholly in the spirit of the stream since we are in it. Let us not stiffen in our innovations! It was not, as you said, "to pick to pieces your form." That we thought the other day. Neither to demand from it "*perfection, as a form.*" But that a pliant medium should be presented for the ever present spirit, not *brittle* but *plastic.*

Tiresome is our life at times, perhaps forlorn, when we would lean on a pillar of strong marble seeking the heavens, and find nothing but a reed. But the wiser mind rejoices that it can noway be excused from constant thought, from an ever springing life, and must in this day stand beneath a naked heaven whose light no dome built by the energy of man is able to intercept.

LETTERS, 1843

When I have been in the country, its beauty has filled me with rapture, but among *men* oh, how lonely! If it is my fault that I have met with so little congenial, it has not been for want of good will. I have earnestly wished to see things as they are, and to appreciate the great influences which are at work here at their just value. But they seem to me to tend so exclusively to bring the riches out of the earth; should that task ever have a long period *exclusively to itself*?...

My friend, I am deeply homesick, yet where is that home? — If not on earth, why should we look to heaven. I would fain truly live wherever I must abide, but with full energy on my lot, whatever it is. He who alone knoweth will affirm that I have tried to work whole hearted, from an earnest faith. Yet my hand is often languid, and my heart is slow. — I must be gone, I feel, but whither? — I know not, if I cannot make this plot of ground yield me corn and roses, famine must be my lot forever and ever surely.

LETTERS, 1843

It was once a beautiful custom among some of the Indian tribes, once a year, to extinguish all the fires, and, by a day of fasting and profound devotion, to propitiate the Great Spirit for the coming year. They then produced sparks by friction, and lit up afresh the altar and the hearth with the new fire.

And this was considered as the most precious and sacred gift from one person to another, binding them in bonds of inviolate friendship for that year, certainly; with a hope that the same might endure through life. From the young to the old it was a token of the highest respect; from the old to the young, of a great expectation.

To us might it be granted to solemnize the new year by the mental renovation of which this ceremony was the eloquent symbol! Might we extinguish, if only for a day, those fires where an uninformed religious ardor has led to human sacrifices; which have warmed the household, but, also, prepared pernicious, more than wholesome, viands for their use.

The Indian produced the new spark by friction. It would be a still more beautiful emblem, and expressive of the more extended powers of civilized men, if we should draw the spark from the centre of our system and the source of light by means of the burning glass.

Where, then, is to be found the new knowledge, the new thought, the new hope, that shall begin a new year in a spirit not discordant with 'the acceptable year of the Lord?' Surely, there must be such existing, if latent — some sparks of new fire, pure from ashes and from smoke, worthy to be offered as a new-year's gift? Let us look at the signs of the times, to see in what spot this fire shall be sought — on what fuel it may be fed. The ancients poured our libations of the choicest juices of Earth, to express their gratitude to the Power that had enabled them to be sustained from her bosom. They enfranchised slaves, to show that devotion to the Gods induced a sympathy with men.

Let us look about us to see with what rites, what acts of devotion, this modern Christian nation greets the approach of the New Year; by what signs she denotes the clear morning of a better day, such as may be expected when the eagle has entered into covenant with the dove!

NEW YEAR'S DAY

I stand in the sunny noon of life. Objects no longer glitter in the dews of morning, neither are yet softened by the shadows of evening. Every spot is seen, every chasm revealed. Climbing the dusty hill, some fair effigies that once stood for symbols of human destiny have been broken; those I still have with me, show defects in this broad light. Yet enough is left, even by experience, to point distinctly to the glories of that destiny; faint, but not to be mistaken streaks of the future day. I can say with the bard,

Though many have suffered shipwreck, still beat noble hearts.

Always the soul says to us all: Cherish your best hopes as a faith, and abide by them in action.

WOMAN IN THE NINETEENTH CENTURY

O awake indeed, Romans! and you will see that the Christ who is to save men is no wooden dingy effigy of bygone superstitions, but such as Art has seen him in your better mood, — a Child, living, full of love, prophetic of a boundless future, — a Man acquainted with all sorrows that rend the heart of all, and ever loving man with sympathy and faith death could not quench, — *that* Christ lives and may be sought; burn your doll of wood.

How any one can remain a Catholic — I mean who has ever been aroused to think, and is not biased by the partialities of childish years — after seeing Catholicism here in Italy, I cannot conceive. There was once a soul in the religion while the blood of its martyrs was yet fresh upon the ground, but that soul was always too much encumbered with the remains of pagan habits and customs: that soul is now quite fled elsewhere, and in the splendid catafalque, watched by so many white and red-robed snuff-taking, sly-eyed men, would they let it be opened, nothing would be found but bones!

THINGS AND THOUGHTS IN EUROPE

There is almost too much of bitter mixed in the cup of life. You say religion is a mere sentiment with you, and that if you are disappointed in your first, your very first hopes and plans, you do not know whether you shall be able to act well. I do not myself see how a reflecting soul can endure the passage through life, except by confidence in a Power that must at last order all things right, and the resolution that it shall not be our own fault if we are not happy, — that we will resolutely deserve to be happy. There are many bright glimpses in life, many still hours; much worthy toil, some deep and noble joys; but, then, there are so many, and such long, intervals, when we are kept from all we want, and must perish but for such thoughts.

LETTERS, N.D.

You know how, when the leadings of my life found their interpretation, I longed to share my joy with those I prized most; for I felt that if they could but understand the past we should meet entirely. They received me, some more, some less, according to the degree of intimacy between our natures. But now I have done with the past, and again move for-

54

ward. The path looks more difficult, but I am better able to bear its trials. We shall have much communion, even if not in the deepest places. I feel no need of isolation, but only of temperance in thought and speech, that the essence may not evaporate in words, but grow plenteous within. The Life will give me to my own. I am not yet so worthy to love as some others are, because my manifold nature is not yet harmonized enough to be faithful, and I begin to see how much it was the want of a pure music in me that has made the good doubt me. Yet have I been true to the best light I had, and if I am so now much will be given.

During my last weeks of solitude I was very happy, and all that had troubled me became clearer. The angel was not weary of waiting for Gunhilde, till she had unraveled her mesh of thought, and seeds of mercy, of purification, were planted in the breast. Whatever the past has been, I feel that I have always been reading on and on, and that the Soul of all souls has been patient in love to mine. New assurances were given me, that if I would be faithful and humble, there was no experience that would not tell its heavenly errand. If shadows have fallen, already they give way to a fairer if more tempered light; and for the present I am so happy that the spirit kneels.

Life is richly worth living, with its continual revelations of mighty woe, yet infinite hope; and I take it to my breast. Amid these scenes of beauty, all that is little, foreign, unworthy, vanishes like a dream. So shall it be some time amidst the Everlasting Beauty when true joy shall begin and never cease.

MEMOIRS

I have been a chosen one; the lesson of renunciation was early, fully taught, and the heart of stone quite broken through. The Great Spirit wished to leave me no refuge but itself. Convictions have been given, enough to guide me many years if I am steadfast. How deeply, how gratefully I feel this blessing, as the fabric of others' hopes are shivering round me. Peace will not always flow thus softly in my life; but, O, our Father! how many hours has He consecrated to Himself. How often has the Spirit chosen the time, when no ray came from without, to descend upon the orphan life!

MEMOIRS

I was in a state of celestial happiness, which lasted a great while. For months I was all radiant with faith, and love, and life. I began to be myself. Night and day were equally beautiful, and the lowest and highest equally holy. Before, it had seemed as if the Divine only gleamed upon me; but then it poured into and through me a tide of light. I have passed down from the rosy mountain, now; but I do not forget its pure air, nor how the storms looked as they rolled beneath my feet. I have received my assurance, and if the shadows should lie upon me for a century, they could never make me forgetful of the true hour. Patiently I bide my time.

MEMOIRS

A New Manifestation

Like many of her friends and fellow Transcendentalists, Margaret Fuller applied her political idealism to the task of improving society. Social conditions for Native Americans, slaves, women, immigrants, the poor, and the incarcerated cried out for "a new manifestation" of the principles on which the nation was established: "While any one is base, none can be entirely free and noble." Entrenched customs and "commercial fever" have debased our institutions and vulgarized the thought of the nation. "The wrongs, woes, and errors of the world yet unredressed," led Fuller to advocate education and action in light of conscience and a higher moral law. The extent of this new manifestation she called for was continually enlarged as her own sphere of involvement widened, from the parlors of Boston to the streets of New York and, finally, to the barricades of Rome.

Yet, no doubt, a new manifestation is at hand, a new hour in the day of man. We cannot expect to see any one sample of completed being, when the mass of men still lie engaged in the sod, or use the freedom of their limbs only with wolfish energy. The tree cannot come to flower till its root be free from the cankering worm, and its whole growth open to air and light. While any one is base, none can be entirely free and noble. Yet something new shall presently be shown of the life of man, for hearts crave, if minds do not know how to ask it.

WOMAN IN THE NINETEENTH CENTURY

Since the Revolution, there has been little, in the circumstances of this country, to call out the higher sentiments. The effect of continued prosperity is the same on nations as on individuals, — it leaves the nobler faculties undeveloped. The need of bringing out the physical resources of a vast extent of country the commercial and political fever incident to our institutions, tend to fix the eyes of men on what is local and temporary, on the external advantages of their condition. The superficial diffusion of knowledge, unless attended by a correspondent deepening of its sources, is likely to vulgarize rather than to raise the thought of a nation, depriving them of another sort of education through sentiments of reverence, and leading the multitude to believe themselves capable of judging what they but dimly discern. They see a wide surface, and forget the difference between seeing and knowing. In this hasty way of thinking and living they traverse so much ground that they forget that not the sleeping railroad passenger, but the botanist, the geologist, the poet, really see the country, and that, to the former, "a miss is as good as a mile." In a word, the tendency of circumstances has been to make our people superficial, irreverent, and more anxious to get a living than to live mentally and morally.

LETTERS, 1840

But of all these plague-spots there is none from which we feel such burning pain of shame and indignation, as from the conduct of this nation toward the Indians. Spoilation, aggression, falsehood of the blackest character, a hundred times repeated, each time with increased shamelessness, mark every step of this intercourse. If good men have sometimes interposed, it is but as a single human arm might strive to stay the torrent. The sense of the nation has been throughout, Might makes Right. We will get what we want at any rate. What does it signify what becomes of the Indians? They are red. They are unlike us in character and person. — Let them save themselves if they can, the Indian dogs.

REVIEW OF THOMAS L. MCKENNEY,
MEMOIRS, OFFICIAL AND PERSONAL

Red Jacket's face, too, is much more intellectual than almost any other. But, in becoming so, it loses nothing of the peculiar Indian stamp, but only carries these traits to their perfection. Irony, discernment, resolution, and a deep smouldering fire, that disdains to flicker where it cannot blaze, may there be read. Nothing can better represent the sort of unfeelingness the whites have towards the Indians, than their conduct towards his remains. He had steadily opposed the introduction of white religion, or manners, among the Indians. He believed that for them to break down the barriers was to perish. On many occasions he had expressed this with all the force of his eloquence. He told the preachers, "if the Great Spirit had meant your religion for the red man, he would have given it to them. What they (the missionaries) tell us, we do not understand; and the light they ask for us, makes the straight and plain path trod by our fathers dark and dreary."

SUMMER ON THE LAKES

I have not wished to write sentimentally about the Indians, however moved by the thought of their wrongs and speedy extinction. I know that the Europeans who took possession of this country, felt themselves justified by their superior civilization and religious ideas. Had they been truly civilized or Christianized, the conflicts which sprang from the collision of the two races, might have been avoided; but this cannot be expected in movements made by masses of men. The mass has never yet been humanized, though the age may develop a human thought.

Since those conflicts and differences did arise, the hatred which sprang, from terror and suffering, on the European side, has naturally warped the whites still farther from justice.

SUMMER ON THE LAKES

Thanksgiving is peculiarly the festival day of New-England. Elsewhere, other celebrations rival its attractions, but in that region where the Puritans first returned thanks that some among them had been sustained by a great hope and earnest resolve amid the perils of the ocean, wild beasts and famine, the old spirit which hallowed the day still lingers, and forbids that it should be entirely devoted to play and plum-pudding . . . .

And for this present day appointed for Thanksgiving, we may say that if we know of so many wrongs, woes, and errors in the world yet unredressed; if in this nation recent decisions have shown a want of moral discrimination on important subjects, that make us pause and doubt whether we can join in the formal congratulations that we are still bodily alive, unassailed by the ruder modes of warfare, and enriched with the fatness of the land; yet on the other side, we know of causes not so loudly proclaimed why we should give thanks. Abundantly and humbly we must render them for the movement, now sensible in the heart of the civilized world, although it has not pervaded the entire frame.

THANKSGIVING

Can he sleep, who in this past year has wickedly or lightly committed acts calculated to injure the few or many — who has poisoned the ears and the hearts he might have rightly informed — who has steeped in tears the cup of thousands — who has put back, as far as in him lay, the accomplishment of general good and happiness for the sake of his selfish aggrandizement or selfish luxury — who has sold to a party what is meant for mankind? If such sleep, dreadful shall be the waking.

Deliver us from evil. In public or in private it is easy to give pain — hard to give pure pleasure; easy to do evil — hard to do good. God does His good in the whole, despite of bad men; but only from a very pure mind will He permit original good to proceed in the day. Happy those who can feel that during the past year, they have, to the best of their knowledge, refrained from evil. Happy those who determine to proceed in this by the light of Conscience. It is but a spark; yet from that spark may be drawn fire-light enough for worlds and systems of worlds, and that light is ever new.

And with this thought rises again the memory of the fair lines that light has brought to view in the histories of some men. If the nation tends to wrong, there are yet present the ten just men. The hands and lips of this great form may be impure, but pure blood flows yet within her veins — the blood of the noble bands who first sought these shores from the British isles and France for conscience sake. Too many have come since for bread alone. We cannot blame — we must not reject them, but let us teach them, in giving them bread, to prize that salt, too, without which all on earth must lose its savor. Yes! let us teach them, not rail at their inevitable ignorance and unenlightened action, but teach them and their children as our own; if we do so, their children and ours may yet act as one body obedient to one soul, and if we should act rightly now, that soul a pure soul.

NEW YEAR'S DAY

To those of us who hate emphasis and exaggeration, who believe that whatever is good of its kind is good, who shrink from love of excitement and love of sway, who, while ready for duties of many kinds, dislike pledges and bonds to any, — this talk about "Woman's Sphere," "Woman's Mission," and all such phrases as mark the present consciousness of an impending transition from old conventions to greater freedom, are most repulsive. And it demands some valor to lift one's head amidst the shower of public squibs, private sneers, anger, scorn, derision, called out by the demand that women should be put on a par with their brethren, legally and politically; that they should hold property not by permission but by right, and that they should take an active part in all great movements . . . . Yet it is plain that we must face this agitation; and beyond the dull clouds overhead hangs in the horizon Venus, as morning-star, no less fair, though of more melting beauty, than the glorious Jupiter, who shares with her the watch.

MEMOIRS

Though the national independence be blurred by the servility of individuals, though freedom and equality have been proclaimed only to leave room for a monstrous display of slave-dealing and slave-keeping; though the free American so often feels himself free, like the Roman, only to pamper his appetites and his indolence through the misery of his fellow beings, still it is not in vain, that the verbal statement has been made, "All men are born free and equal." There it stands, a golden certainty wherewith to encourage the good, to shame the bad. The new world may be called clearly to perceive that it incurs the utmost penalty, if it reject or oppress the sorrowful brother. And, if men are deaf, the angels hear. But men cannot be deaf. It is inevitable that an external freedom, an independence of the encroachments of other men, such as has been achieved for the nation, should be so also for every member of it. That which has once been clearly conceived in the intelligence cannot fail sooner or later to be acted out. It has become a law as irrevocable as that of the Medes in their ancient dominion . . . .

This law cannot fail of universal recognition. Accursed be he who willingly saddens an immortal spirit, doomed to infamy in later, wiser ages, doomed in future stages of his own being to deadly penance, only short of death. Accursed be he who sins in ignorance, if that ignorance be caused by sloth.

WOMAN IN THE NINETEENTH CENTURY

While it is the destiny of Man, in the course of the Ages, to ascertain and fulfill the law of his being, so that his life shall be seen, as a whole, to be that of an angel or messenger, the action of prejudices and passions, which attend, in the day, the growth of the individual, is continually obstructing the holy work that is to make the earth a part of heaven. By Man I mean both man and woman: these are the two halves of one thought. I lay no especial stress on the welfare of either. I believe that the development of the one cannot be effected without that of the other. My highest wish is that this truth should be distinctly and rationally apprehended, and the conditions of life and freedom recognized as the same for the daughters and the sons of time; twin exponents of a divine thought.

WOMAN IN THE NINETEENTH CENTURY

Meanwhile not a few believe, and men themselves have expressed the opinion, that the time is come when Eurydice is to call for an Orpheus, rather than Orpheus for Eurydice: that the idea of Man, however imperfectly brought out, has been far more so than that of Woman, that she, the other half of the same thought, the other chamber of the heart of life, needs now to take her turn in the full pulsation, and that improvement in the daughters will best aid in the reformation of the sons of this age.

It should be remarked that, as the principle of liberty is better understood, and more nobly interpreted, a broader protest is made in behalf of Woman. As men become aware that few men have had a fair chance, they are inclined to say that no women have had a fair chance.

WOMAN IN THE NINETEENTH CENTURY

Yet, by men in this country, as by the Jews, when Moses was leading them to the promised land, every thing has been done that inherited depravity could do, to hinder the promise of heaven from its fulfillment. The cross here as elsewhere, has been planted only to be blasphemed by cruelty and fraud. The name of the Prince of Peace has been profaned by all kinds of injustice toward the Gentile whom he said he came to save. But I need not speak of what has been done towards the red man, the black man, Those deeds are the scoff of the world; and they have been accompanied by such pious words that the gentlest would not dare to intercede with "Father, forgive them, for they know not what they do."

WOMAN IN THE NINETEENTH CENTURY

Knowing that there exists in the minds of men a tone of feeling towards women as towards slaves, such as is expressed in the common phrase, "Tell that to women and children," that the infinite soul can only work through them in already ascertained limits; that the gift of reason, man's highest prerogative, is allotted to them in much lower degree; that they must be kept from mischief and melancholy by being constantly engaged in active labor, which is to be furnished and directed by those better able to think, &c. &c.; we need not multiply instances, for who can review the experience of last week without recalling words which imply, whether in jest or earnest, these views or views like these; knowing this, can we wonder that many reformers think that measures are not likely to be taken in behalf of women, unless their wishes could be publicly represented by women?

WOMAN IN THE NINETEENTH CENTURY

As to men's representing women fairly at present, while we hear from men who owe to their wives not only all that is comfortable or graceful, but all that is wise in the arrangement of their lives, the frequent remark, "You cannot reason with a woman," when from those of delicacy, nobleness, and poetic culture, the contemptuous phrase "women and children," and that in no light sally of the hour, but in works intended to give a permanent statement of the best experiences, when not one man, in the million, shall I say? no, not in the hundred million, can rise above the belief that woman was made *for man*, when such traits as these are daily forced upon the attention, can we feel that man will always do justice to the interests of woman? Can we think that he takes a sufficiently discerning and religious view of her office and destiny, *ever* to do her justice, except when prompted by sentiment, accidentally or transiently, that is, for the sentiment will vary according to the relations in which he is placed. The lover, the poet, the artist, are likely to view her nobly. The father and the philosopher have some chance of liberality; the man of the world, the legislator for expediency, none.

WOMAN IN THE NINETEENTH CENTURY

We would have every arbitrary barrier thrown down. We would have every path laid open to woman as freely as to man. Were this done and a slight temporary fermentation allowed to subside, we should see crystallizations more pure and of more various beauty. We believe the divine energy would pervade nature to a degree unknown in the history of former ages, and that no discordant collision, but a ravishing harmony of the spheres would ensue.

Yet, then and only then, will mankind be ripe for this, when inward and outward freedom for woman as much as for man shall be acknowledged as a right, not yielded as a concession. As the friend of the negro assumes that one man cannot by right, hold another in bondage, so should the friend of woman assume that man cannot, by right, lay even well-meant restrictions on woman. If the negro be a soul, if the woman be a soul, appareled in flesh, to one Master only are they accountable. There is but one law for souls, and if there is to be an interpreter of it, he must come not as man, or son of man, but as son of God.

WOMAN IN THE NINETEENTH CENTURY

Mysticism, which may be defined as the brooding soul of the world, cannot fail of its oracular promise as to woman. "The mothers" — "The mother of all things," are expressions of thought which lead the mind towards this side of universal growth. Whenever a mystical whisper was heard, from Behmen down to St. Simon, sprang up the thought, that, if it be true, as the legend says, that humanity withers through a fault committed by and a curse laid upon woman, through her pure child, or influence, shall the new Adam, the redemption, arise.

WOMAN IN THE NINETEENTH CENTURY

The especial genius of woman I believe to be electrical in movement, intuitive in function, spiritual in tendency. She excels not so easily in classification, or re-creation, as in an instinctive seizure of causes, and a simple breathing out of what she receives that has the singleness of life, rather than the selecting and energizing of art.

More native is it to her to be the living model of he artist than to set apart from herself any one form in objective reality; more native to inspire and receive the poem, than to create it. In so far as soul is in her completely developed, all soul is the same; but as far as it is modified in her as woman, it flows, it breathes, it sings, rather than deposits soil, or finishes work, and that which is especially feminine flushes, in blossom, the face of earth, and pervades, like air and water, all this seeming solid globe, daily renewing and purifying its life. Such may be the especially feminine element, spoken of as Femality. But it is no more the order of nature that it should be incarnated pure in any form, than that the masculine energy should exist unmingled with it in any form.

WOMAN IN THE NINETEENTH CENTURY

Male and female represent the two sides of the great radical dualism. But, in fact, they are perpetually passing into one another. Fluid hardens to solid, solid rushes to fluid. There is no wholly masculine man, no purely feminine woman.

History jeers at the attempts of physiologists to bind great original laws by the forms which flow from them. They make a rule; they say from observation, what can and cannot be. In vain! Nature provides exceptions to every rule. She sends women to battle, and sets Hercules spinning; she enables woman to bear immense burdens, cold, and frost; she enables the man, who feels maternal love, to nourish his infant like a mother. Of late she plays still gayer pranks. Not only she deprives organizations, but organs, of a necessary end. She enables people to read with the top of the head, and see with the pit of the stomach. Presently she will make a female Newton, and a male Syren.

WOMAN IN THE NINETEENTH CENTURY

O men! I speak not to you. It is true that your wickedness (for you must not deny that, at least, nine thousand out of the ten fall through the vanity you have systematically flattered, or the promises you have treacherously broken;) yes, it is true that your wickedness is its own punishment. Your forms degraded and your eyes clouded by secret sin; natural harmony broken and fineness of perception destroyed in your mental and bodily organization; God and love shut out from your hearts by the foul visitants you have permitted there; incapable of pure marriage; incapable of pure parentage; incapable of worship; oh wretched men, your sin is its own punishment! You have lost the world in losing yourselves. Who ruins another has admitted the worm to the root of his own tree, and the fuller ye fill the cup of evil, the deeper must be your own bitter draught. But I speak not to you — you need to teach and warn one another. And more than one voice rises in earnestness. And all that *women* say to the heart that has once chosen the evil path, is considered prudery, or ignorance, or perhaps, a feebleness of nature which exempts from similar temptations.

But to you, women, American women, a few words may not be addressed in vain. One here and there may listen.

WOMAN IN THE NINETEENTH CENTURY

The growth of man is two-fold, masculine and feminine.
As far as these two methods can be distinguished they are so as
Energy and Harmony.
Power and Beauty.
Intellect and Love.

Or by some such rude classification, for we have not language primitive and pure enough to express such ideas with precision.

These two sides are supposed to be expressed in man and woman, that is, as the more and less, for the faculties have not been given pure to either, but only in preponderance. There are also exceptions in great number, such as men of far more beauty than power, and the reverse. But as a general rule, it seems to have been the intention to give a preponderance on the one side, that is called masculine, and on the other, one that is called feminine.

There cannot be a doubt that, if these two developments were in perfect harmony, they would correspond to and fulfill one another, like hemispheres, or the tenor and bass in music.

But there is no perfect harmony in human nature; and the two parts answer one another only now and then, or, if there be a persistent consonance, it can only be traced, at long intervals, instead of discoursing an obvious melody.

WOMAN IN THE NINETEENTH CENTURY

I have aimed to show that no age was left entirely without a witness of the equality of the sexes in function, duty and hope.

Also that, when there was unwillingness or ignorance, which prevented this being acted upon, women had not the less power for their want of light and noble freedom. But it was power which hurt alike them and those against whom they made use of the arms of the servile; cunning, blandishment, and unreasonable emotion.

That now the time has come when a clearer vision and better action are possible. When man and woman may regard one another as brother and sister, the pillars of one porch, the priests of one worship.

I have believed and intimated that this hope would receive an ampler fruition, than ever before, in our own land.

And it will do so if this land carry out the principles from which sprang our national life.

I believe that, at present, women are the best helpers of one another.

Let them think; let them act; till they know what they need.

We only ask of men to remove arbitrary barriers. Some would like to do more. But I believe it needs for woman to show herself in her native dignity, to teach them how to aid her; their minds are so encumbered by tradition.

WOMAN IN THE NINETEENTH CENTURY

Woman, self-centred, would never be absorbed by any relation; it would be only an experience to her as to man. It is a vulgar error that love, *a* love to woman is her whole existence; she also is born for Truth and Love in their universal energy. Would she but assume her inheritance, Mary would not be the only virgin mother. Not Manzoni alone would celebrate in his wife the virgin mind with the maternal wisdom and conjugal affections. The soul is ever young, ever virgin.

And will not she soon appear? The woman who shall vindicate their birthright for all women; who shall teach them what to claim, and how to use what they obtain? Shall not her name be for her era Victoria, for her country and life Virginia? Yet predictions are rash; she herself must teach us to give her the fitting name.

WOMAN IN THE NINETEENTH CENTURY

Much has been written about Woman's keeping within her sphere, which is defined as the domestic sphere. As a little girl she is to learn the lighter family duties, while she acquires that limited acquaintance with the realm of literature and science that will enable her to superintend the instruction of children in their earliest years. It is not generally proposed that she should be sufficiently instructed and developed to understand the pursuits or aims of her future husband; she is not to be a helpmeet to him, in the way of companionship or counsel, except in the care of his house and children. Her youth is to be passed partly in learning to keep house and the use of the needle, partly in the social circle where her manners may be formed, ornamental accomplishments perfected and displayed, and the husband found who shall give her the domestic sphere for which exclusively she is to be prepared . . . .

But the most fastidious critic on the departure of Woman from her sphere, can scarcely fail to see at present that a vast proportion of the sex, if not the better half, do not, cannot, have this domestic sphere.

Thousands and scores of thousands in this country no less than in Europe are obliged to maintain themselves alone. Far greater numbers divide with their husbands the care of earning a support for the family. In England, now, the progress of society has reached so admirable a pitch that the position of the sexes is frequently reversed, and the husband is obliged to stay at home and "mind the house and bairns" while the wife goes forth to the employment she alone can secure.

THE WRONGS OF AMERICAN WOMEN.
THE DUTY OF AMERICAN WOMEN.

Had Christendom but been true to its standard, while accommodating its modes of operation to the calls of successive times, Woman would now have not only equal *power* with Man, — for of that omnipotent nature will never suffer her to be defrauded, — but a *chartered* power, too fully recognized to be abused. Indeed, all that is wanting is, that Man should prove his own freedom by making her free. Let him abandon conventional restriction, as a vestige of that Oriental barbarity which confined Woman to a seraglio. Let him trust her entirely, and give her every privilege already acquired for himself, — elective franchise, tenure of property, liberty to speak in public assemblies, &c.

EDUCATE MEN AND WOMEN AS SOULS

Much has been achieved in this country since the first Declaration of Independence. America is rich and strong; she has shown great talent and energy; vast prospects of aggrandizement open before her. But the noble sentiment which she expressed in her early youth is tarnished; she has shown that righteousness is not her chief desire, and her name is no longer a watchword for the highest hopes to the rest of the world. She knows this, but takes it very easily; she feels that she is growing richer and more powerful, and that seems to suffice her.

These facts are deeply saddening to those who can pronounce the words 'My Country' with pride and peace only so far as steadfast virtues, generous impulses find their home in that country. They cannot be satisfied with superficial benefits, with luxuries and the means of obtaining knowledge which are multiplied for them. They could rejoice in full hands and a busy brain, if the soul were expanding and the heart pure, but, the higher conditions being violated, what is done cannot be done for good.

FOURTH OF JULY

The aspect of Nature was sad; what is worse, it was dull and dubious, when we set forth on these visits. The sky was leaden and lowering, the air unkind and piercing, the little birds sat mute and astonished at the departure of the beautiful days which had lured them to premature song. It was a suitable day for such visits. The pauper establishments that belong to a great city take the place of the skeleton at the banquets of old. They admonish us of stern realities, which must bear the same explanation as the frequent blight of Nature's bloom. They should be looked at by all, if only for their own sakes, that they may not sink listlessly into selfish ease, in a world so full of disease. They should be looked at by all who wish to enlighten themselves as to the means of aiding their fellow creatures in any way, public or private. For nothing can really be done till the right principles are discovered, and it would seem they still need to be discovered or elucidated, so little is done, with a great deal of desire in the heart of the community to do what is right. Such visits are not yet calculated to encourage and exhilarate, as does the story of the Prodigal Son; they wear a grave aspect and suit the grave mood of a *cold* Spring day.

OUR CITY CHARITIES

Dear Public and Friends! we wish you a happy New Year. We trust that the year past has given earnest of such an one in so far as having taught you somewhat how to deserve and to appreciate it.

For ourselves the months have brought much, though, perhaps, superficial instruction. Its scope has been chiefly Love and Hope for all human beings, and among others for thyself.

We have seen many fair poesies of human life, in which, however, the tragic thread has not been wanting. We have seen the exquisite developments of childhood and sunned the heart in its smiles. But also we have seen the evil star looming up that threatened cloud and wreck to its future years. We have seen beings of some precious gifts lost irre-coverably as regards this present life from inheritance of a bad orga-nization and unfortunate circumstances of early years. We have seen the victims of vice lying in the gutter, companied by vermin, trampled upon by sensuality and ignorance. We have seen those who wished not to rise, and those who strove to do so, but fell back through weakness. Sadder and more ominous still, we have seen the good man — in many impulses and acts of most pure, most liberal, and undoubted goodness — we have seen a spot of base indulgence, a fibre of brutality, canker in a vital part of this fine plant, and, while we could not withdraw love and esteem for the good we could not doubt, have wept secretly in the corner for the ill we could not deny . . . .

But for ourselves, we find there is kernel in the nut, though its rip-ening be deferred till the late frosty weather, and it prove a hard nut to crack, even then. Looking at the individual, we see a degree of growth, or the promise of such. In the child there is a force which will outlast the wreck and reach at last the promised shore. The good man, once roused from his moral lethargy, shall make atonement for his fault, and endure a penance that will deepen and purify his whole nature. The poor lost ones claim a new trial in a new life, and will there, we trust, seize firmer hold on the good for the experience they have had of the bad.

1ST JANUARY, 1846

On Sunday [the prisoners at Sing Sing] are all confined in their cells after 12 at noon that their keepers may have rest from their weekly fatigues, but I was allowed to have some of the women out to talk with and the interview was very pleasant. They were among the so called worst, but nothing could be more decorous than their conduct, and frank too. All passed much as in one of my Boston Classes. I told them I was writing about Woman and as my path had been a favoured one I wanted to ask some information of those who had been tempted to pollution and sorrow. They seemed to reply in the same spirit in which I asked. Several however expressed a wish to see me alone, as they could then say *all*, and they could not bear to before one another; and I intend to go there again, and take the time for this.

LETTERS, 1844

Go to the Penitentiary at Blackwell's Island. You may be repelled by seeing those who are in health, while at work together, keeping up one another's careless spirit and effrontery by bad association. But see them in the hospital where the worn features of the sick show the sad ruins of past loveliness, past gentleness. See in the eyes of the nurses the woman's spirit still, so kindly, so inspiring. See those little girls huddled in a corner, their neglected dress and hair contrasting with some ribbon of cherished finery held fast in a childish hand. Think what "sweet seventeen" was to you, and what it is to them, and see if you do not wish to aid in any enterprise that gives them a chance of better days. We assume no higher claim for this enterprise. The dreadful social malady which creates the need of it is one that imperatively demands deep-searching preventive measures; it is beyond cure. But, here and there, some precious soul may be saved from unwilling sin, unutterable woe. Is not the hope to save, here and there *one*, worthy of great and persistent exertion and sacrifice?

ASYLUM FOR DISCHARGED FEMALE CONVICTS

Passing to the Penitentiary, we entered on one of the gloomiest scenes that deforms this great metropolis . . . .

The want of proper matrons, or any matrons, to take the care so necessary for the bodily or mental improvement or even decent condition of the seven hundred women assembled here, is an offence that cries aloud. It is impossible to take the most cursory survey of this assembly of women; especially it is impossible to see them in the Hospital, where the circumstances are a little more favorable, without seeing how many there are in whom the feelings of innocent childhood are not dead, who need only good influences and steady aid to raise them from the pit of infamy and woe into which they have fallen. And, if there was not one that could be helped, at least Society owes them the insurance of a decent condition while here. We trust that interest on this subject will not slumber.

The recognized principles of all such institutions which have any higher object than the punishment of fault, (and we believe few among us are so ignorant as to avow that as the only object, though they may, from want of thought, act as if it were,) are — Classification as the first step, that the bad may not impede those who wish to do well; 2d. Instruction, practical, oral, and by furnishing books which may open entirely new hopes and thoughts to minds oftener darkened than corrupted; 3d. A good Sanitary system, which promotes self-respect, and, through health and purity of body, the same in mind.

OUR CITY CHARITIES

When we consider all the fire which glows so untameably in Irish veins, the character of her people, considering the circumstances — almost miraculous in its goodness — we cannot forbear, notwithstanding all the temporary ills they aid in here, to give them all a welcome to our shores. Those ills we need not enumerate; they are known to all, and we rank among them what others would not, that by their ready service to do all the hard work they make it easier for the rest of the population to grow effeminate and help the country to grow too fast. But that is her destiny, to grow too fast; it is useless talking against it. Their extreme ignorance, their blind devotion to a priesthood, the pliancy in the hands of demagogues threaten continuance of these ills; yet, on the other hand, we must regard them as a most valuable element in the new race. They are looked upon with contempt for their want of aptitude at learning new things, their ready and ingenious lying, their eye service. These are the faults of an oppressed race which must require the aid of better circumstances through two or three generations to eradicate. Their virtues are their own; — they are many, genuine, and deeply rooted. Can an impartial observer fail to admire their truth to domestic ties, their power of generous bounty and more generous gratitude, their indefatigable good humor, (for ages of wrong, which have driven them to so many acts of desperation, could never sour their blood at its source,) their ready wit, their elasticity of nature. They are at bottom one of the best nations of the world. — Would they were welcomed here, not to work merely, but to intelligent sympathy and efforts, both patient and ardent for the education of their children. No sympathy could be better deserved, no efforts wiselier timed.

THE IRISH CHARACTER

73

Farewell to New York city, where twenty months have presented me with a richer and more varied exercise for thought and life, than twenty years could in any other part of these United States.

It is the common remark about New York, that it has at least nothing petty or provincial in its methods and habits. The place is large enough: there is room enough, and occupation enough, for men to have no need or excuse for small cavils or scrutinies. A person who is independent, and knows what he wants, may lead his proper life here, unimpeded by others.

Vice and crime, if flagrant and frequent, are less thickly coated by hypocrisy than elsewhere. The air comes sometimes to the most infected subjects.

New York is the focus, the point where American and European interests converge. There is no topic of general interest to men, that will not betimes be brought before the thinker by the quick turning of the wheel . . . .

I go to behold the wonders of art, and the temples of old religion. But I shall see no forms of beauty and majesty beyond what my country is capable of producing in myriad variety, if she has but the soul to will it; no temple to compare with what she might erect in the ages, if the catchword of the time, a sense of *divine order*, should become no more a mere word of form, but a deeply rooted and pregnant idea in her life. Beneath the light of a hope that this may be, I say to my friends once more a kind farewell!

FAREWELL

In the spring, when I came to Rome, the people were in the intoxication of joy at the first serious measures of reform taken by the Pope. I saw with pleasure their childlike joy and trust. With equal pleasure I saw the Pope, who has not in his expression the signs of intellectual greatness so much as of nobleness and tenderness of heart, of large and liberal sympathies. Heart had spoken to heart between the prince and the people; it was beautiful to see the immediate good influence exerted by human feeling and generous designs, on the part of a ruler. He had wished to be a father, and the Italians, with that readiness of genius that characterizes them, entered at once into the relation; they, the Roman people, stigmatized by prejudice as so crafty and ferocious, showed themselves children, eager to learn, quick to obey, happy to confide.

Still doubts were always present whether all this joy was not premature. The task undertaken by the Pope seemed to present insuperable difficulties. It is never easy to put new wine into old bottles, and our age is one where all things tend to a great crisis; not merely to revolution, but to radical reform. From the people themselves the help must come, and not from princes; in the new state of things, there will be none but natural princes, great men. From the aspirations of the general heart, from the teachings of conscience in individuals, and not from an old ivy-covered church long since undermined, corroded by time and gnawed by vermin, the help must come. Rome, to resume her glory, must cease to be an ecclesiastical capital; must renounce all this gorgeous mummery, whose poetry, whose picture, charms no one more than myself, but whose meaning is all of the past and finds no echo in the future.

THINGS AND THOUGHTS IN EUROPE

Eighteen hundred years of this Christian culture in these European kingdoms, a great theme never lost sight of, a mighty idea, an adorable history to which the hearts of men invariably cling, yet are genuine results rare as grains of gold in the river's sandy bed! Where is the genuine democracy to which the rights of all men are holy? where the child-like wisdom learning all through life more and more of the will of God? where the aversion to falsehood, in all its myriad disguises of cant, vanity, covetousness, so clear to be read in all the history of Jesus of Nazareth? Modern Europe is the sequel to that history, and see this hollow England, with its monstrous wealth and cruel poverty, its conventional life, and low, practical aims! see this poor France, so full of talent, so adroit, yet so shallow and glossy still, which could not escape from a false position with all its baptism of blood! see that lost Poland, and this Italy bound down by treacherous hands in all the force of genius! see Russia with its brutal Czar and innumerable slaves! see Austria and its royalty that represents nothing, and its people, who, as people, are and have nothing! If we consider the amount of truth that has really been spoken out in the world, and the love that has beat in

75

private hearts, — how genius has decked each spring-time with such splendid flowers, conveying each one enough of instruction in its life of harmonious energy, and how continually, unquenchably, the spark of faith has striven to burst into flame and light up the universe, — the public failure seems amazing, seems monstrous.

THINGS AND THOUGHTS IN EUROPE

Can I say our social laws are generally better, or show a nobler insight into the wants of man and woman? I do, indeed, say what I believe, that voluntary association for improvement in these particulars will be the grand means for my nation to grow, and give a nobler harmony to the coming age. But it is only of a small minority that I can say they as yet seriously take to heart these things; that they earnestly meditate on what is wanted for their country, for mankind, — for our cause is indeed the cause of all mankind at present. Could we succeed, really succeed, combine a deep religious love with practical development, the achievements of genius with the happiness of the multitude, we might believe man had now reached a commanding point in his ascent, and would stumble and faint no more. Then there is this horrible cancer of slavery, and the wicked war that has grown out of it. How dare I speak of these things here? I listen to the same arguments against the emancipation of Italy that are used against the emancipation of our blacks; the same arguments in favor of the spoliation of Poland, as for the conquest of Mexico. I find the cause of tyranny and wrong everywhere the same, — and lo! my country! the darkest offender, because with the least excuse; forsworn to the high calling with which she was called; no champion of the rights of men, but a robber and a jailer; the scourge hid behind her banner; her eyes fixed, not on the stars, but on the possessions of other men.

THINGS AND THOUGHTS IN EUROPE

It is to the youth that Hope addresses itself; to those who yet burn with aspiration, who are not hardened in their sins. But I dare not expect too much of them. I am not very old; yet of those who, in life's morning, I saw touched by the light of a high hope, many have seceded.

Some have become voluptuaries; some, mere family men, who think it quite life enough to win bread for half a dozen people, and treat them decently; others are lost through indolence and vacillation. Yet some remain constant;

I have witnessed many a shipwreck,
Yet still beat noble hearts.

I have found many among the youth of England, of France, of Italy, also, full of high desire; but will they have courage and purity to fight the battle through in the sacred, the immortal band? Of some of them I believe it, and await the proof. If a few succeed amid the trial, we have not lived and loved in vain.

THINGS AND THOUGHTS IN EUROPE

I see you have meetings, where you speak of the Italians, the Hungarians. I pray you *do something*; let it not end in a mere cry of sentiment. That is better than to sneer at all that is liberal, like the English, — than to talk of the holy victims of patriotism as "anarchists" and "brigands"; but it is not enough. It ought not to content your consciences. Do you owe no tithe to Heaven for the privileges it has showered on you, for whose achievement so many here suffer and perish daily? Deserve to retain them, by helping your fellow men to acquire them. Our government must abstain from interference, but private action is practicable, is due. For Italy, it is in this moment too late; but all that helps Hungary helps her also, — helps all who wish the freedom of men from an hereditary yoke now become intolerable. Send money, send cheer, — acknowledge as the legitimate leaders and rulers those men who represent the people, who understand their wants, who are ready to die or to live for their good . . . . Friends, countrymen, and lovers of virtue, lovers of freedom, lovers of truth! be on the alert; rest not supine in your easier lives, but remember

Mankind is one,
And beats with one great heart.

THINGS AND THOUGHTS IN EUROPE

These My Contemporaries

As we have seen, Margaret Fuller was a central figure in the Transcendentalist movement, and a close friend of Emerson, Thoreau, and other Transcendentalists with whom she corresponded, including James Freeman Clarke and William Henry Channing. And as a literary critic, she engaged with the great writers and visionaries of her time. Her relationships with her contemporaries were often intense and demanding. She held them to as high a standard as she held herself. Yet it is clear that Fuller regarded the thoughtfulness and idealism of such people as key to her own growth and the upward progression of humanity, even when she disagreed with their conclusions.

For the past year or two I begin to see a change in the forms of these my contemporaries who have filled my eye. It is a sight that makes me pensive, but awakens, I think, a deeper tenderness and even a higher hope than did these forms in the greatest perfection they ever attained. For they still only promised beauty not gave it, and now seeing the swift changes of time I feel what an illusion all ill, all imperfection is. As they fail to justify my expectation, it only rises the higher and they become dearer as the heralds of a great fulfillment. The princely crest is lowered, the proud glow of youth, its haughty smile and gleaming sweetness are fled, every languid motion assures me that this life will not complete the picture I had sketched, but I only postpone it for ages, and expect it on the same canvass yet.

LETTERS, 1841

As to transcendentalism and the nonsense which is talked by so many about it — I do not know what is meant. For myself I should say that if it is meant that I have an active mind frequently busy with large topics I hope it is so — If it is meant that I am honored by the friendship of such men as Mr. Emerson, Mr. Ripley, or Mr. Alcott, I hope it is so — *But* if it is meant that I cherish any opinions which interfere with domestic duties, cheerful courage and judgment in the practical affairs of life, I challenge any or all in the little world which knows me to prove such deficiency from any acts of mine since I came to woman's estate.

LETTERS, 1837

Mr. Emerson works five or six hours a day in his garden and his health which was in a very low state this spring improves day by day. He has a friend with him of the name of Henry Thoreau who has come to live with him and be his working-man this year. H.T. is three and twenty, has been through college and kept a school, is very fond of classic studies, and an earnest thinker yet intends being a farmer. He has a great deal of practical sense, and as he has bodily strength to boot, he may look to be a successful and happy man. He has a boat which he made himself, and rows me out on the pond. Last night I went out quite late and staid til the moon was almost gone, heard the whip-poor-will for the first time this year. There was a sweet breeze full of appleblossom fragrance which made the pond swell almost into waves. I had great pleasure.

LETTERS, 1841

After the first excitement of intimacy with [Emerson], — when I was made so happy by his high tendency, absolute purity, the freedom and infinite graces of an intellect cultivated much beyond any I had known, — came with me the questioning season. I was greatly disappointed in my relation to him. I was, indeed, always called on to be worthy, this benefit was sure in our friendship. But I found no intelligence of my best self; far less was it revealed to me in new modes; for not only did he seem to want the living faith which enables one to discharge this holiest office of a friend, but he absolutely distrusted me in every region of my life with which he was unacquainted. The same trait I detected in his relations with others. He had faith in the Universal, but not in the Individual Man; he met men, not as a brother, but as a critic. Philosophy appeared to chill instead of exalting the poet.

But now I am better acquainted with him. His "accept" is true; the "I shall learn," with which he answers every accusation, is no less true. No one can feel his limitations, in fact, more than he, though he always speaks confidently from his present knowledge as all he has yet, and never qualifies or explains. He feels himself "shut up in a crystal cell," from which only "a great love or a great task could release me," and hardly expects either from what remains in this life. But I already see so well how these limitations have fitted him for his peculiar work, that I can no longer quarrel with them; while from his eyes looks out the angel that must sooner or later break every chain. Leave him in his cell affirming absolute truth; protesting against humanity, if so he appears to do; the calm observer of the courses of things. Surely, "he keeps true to his thought, which is the great matter." He has already paid his debt to his time; how much more he will give we cannot know; but already I feel how invaluable is a cool mind, like his, amid the warring elements around us. As I look at him more by his own law, I understand him better; and as I understand him better, differences melt away. My inmost heart blesses the fate that gave me birth in the same clime and time, and that has drawn me into such a close bond with him as, it is my hopeful faith, will never be broken, but from sphere to sphere ever more hallowed.

What did you mean by saying I had imbibed much of his way of thought? I do indeed feel his life stealing gradually into mine; and I sometimes think that my work would have been more simple, and my unfolding to a temporal activity more rapid and easy, if we had never met. But when I look forward to eternal growth, I am always aware that I am far larger and deeper for him. His influence has been to me that of lofty assurance and sweet serenity . . . . With most men I bring words of now past life, and do actions suggested by the wants of their natures rather than my own. But he stops me from doing anything, and makes me think.

LETTERS, 1842

You question me as to the nature of the benefits conferred upon me by Mr. E[merson's] preaching. I answer, that his influence has been more beneficial to me than that of any American, and that from him I first learned what is meant by an inward life. Many other springs have since fed the stream of living waters, but he first opened the fountain. That the "mind is its own place," was a dead phrase to me, till he cast light upon my mind. Several of his sermons stand apart in memory, like landmarks of my spiritual history. It would take a volume to tell what this one influence did for me. But perhaps I shall some time see that it was best for me to be forced to help myself.

MEMOIRS

Things go on pretty well, but doubtless people will be disappointed, for they seem to be looking for the Gospel of Transcendentalism . . . . Mr. Emerson knows best what he wants; but he has already said it in various ways. Yet, this experiment is well worth trying; hearts beat so high, they must be full of something, and here is a way to breathe it out quite freely. It is for dear New England that I want this review [the *Dial*]. For myself, if I had wished to write a few pages now and then, there were ways and means enough of disposing of them. But in truth I have not much to say; for since I have had leisure to look at myself, I find that, so far from being an original genius, I have not yet learned to think to any depth, and that the utmost I have done in life has been to form my character to a certain consistency, cultivate my tastes, and learn to tell the truth with a little better grace than I did at first. For this the world will not care much, so I shall hazard a few critical remarks only, or an unpretending chalk sketch now and then, till I have learned to do something.

MEMOIRS

But Waldo's oration ["Emancipation in the British West Indies"], O that was great heroic, calm, sweet, fair. All aspects melted and rendered into one, an archetypal face of the affair. So beautifully spoken too! Better than he ever spoke before: it was true happiness to hear him; tears came to my eyes. The old story of how the blacks received their emancipation: it seemed as if I had never heard before: he gave it such expression. How ashamed one felt ever to be sad, while possessing that degree of freedom which gave them such joy. I felt excited to new life and a nobler emulation by Waldo this day. Yes: it is deeply tragic on the one side, my relation to him, but on the other, how noble how dear! If not an immortal relation, it makes me more immortal. Let me keep both sides duly balanced in my mind. Let me once know him and I shall not be disappointed. But he is hard to know, the subtle Greek!

JOURNAL, 1844

The event of which this day is the anniversary, affords a sufficient guaranty of the safety and practicability of strong measures for this purification. Various accounts are given to the public of the state of the British West Indies, and the foes of emancipation are of course constantly on the alert to detect any unfavorable result which may aid them in opposing the good work elsewhere. But through all statements these facts shine clear as the Sun at noonday, that the measure was there carried into effect with an ease and success, and has shown in the African race a degree of goodness, docility, capacity for industry and self-culture, entirely beyond or opposed to the predictions which darkened so many minds with fears. Those fears can never again be entertained or uttered with the same excuse. One great example of the *safety of doing right* exists; true, there is but one of the sort, but volumes may be preached from such a text.

We, however, preach not; there are too many preachers already in the field, abler, more deeply devoted to the cause. Endless are the sermons of these modern crusaders, those ardent "sons of thunder," who have pledged themselves never to stop or falter till this one black spot be purged away from the land which gave them birth. They cry aloud and spare not; they spare not others, but then, neither do they spare themselves, and such are ever the harbingers of a new advent of the Holy Spirit. Our venerated friend, Dr. Channing, sainted in more memories than any man who has left us in this nineteenth century, uttered the last of his tones of soft, solemn, persuasive, convincing elo-quence on this day and on this occasion. The hills of Lenox laughed and were glad as they heard him who showed in that last address, an address not only to the men of Lenox, but to all men, for he was in the highest sense the Friend of Man, the unsullied purity of infancy, the indignation of youth at vice and wrong, informed and tempered by the mild wisdom of age. It is a beautiful fact, that this should have been the last public occasion of his life.

Last year a noble address was delivered by R. W. Emerson, in which he broadly showed the *juste milieu* views upon this subject in the holy light of a high ideal day. The truest man grew more true as he listened, for the speech, though it had the force of fact and the lustre of thought, was chiefly remarkable as sharing the penetrating quality of the "still, small voice," most often heard when no man speaks. Now it spoke *through* a man, and no personalities, or prejudices, or passions, could be perceived to veil or disturb its silver sound.

FIRST OF AUGUST, 1845

Douglass himself seems very just and temperate. We feel that his view, even of those who have injured him most, may be relied upon. He knows how to allow for motives and influences. Upon the subject of Religion, he speaks with great force, and not more than our own sympathies can respond to. The inconsistencies of Slaveholding professors of religion cry to Heaven. We are not disposed to detest, or refuse communion with them. Their blindness is but one form of that prevalent fallacy which substitutes a creed for a faith, a ritual for a life. We have seen too much of this system of atonement not to know that those who adopt it often began with good intentions, and are, at any rate, in their mistakes worthy of the deepest pity. But that is no reason why the truth should not be uttered, trumpet-tongued, about the thing. "Bring no more vain oblations"; sermons must daily be preached anew on that text. Kings, five hundred years ago, built Churches with the spoils of War; Clergymen to-day command Slaves to obey a Gospel which they will not allow them to read, and call themselves Christians amid the curses of their fellow men. — The world ought to get on a little faster than that, if there be really any principle of improvement in it. The Kingdom of Heaven may not at the beginning have dropped seed larger than a mustard-seed, but even from that we had a right to expect a fuller growth than can be believed to exist, when we read such a book as this of Douglass.

REVIEW OF THE NARRATIVE OF THE LIFE OF FREDRICK DOUGLASS

Would your heart, could you but investigate the matter, approve such overstatement, such a crude, intemperate tirade as you have been guilty of about Mr. Alcott, — a true and noble man, a philanthropist, whom a true and noble woman, also a philanthropist, should have delighted to honor; whose disinterested and resolute efforts, for the redemption of poor humanity, all independent and faithful minds should sustain, since the "broadcloth" vulgar will be sure to assail them; a philosopher, worthy of the palmy times of ancient Greece; a man whom Carlyle and Berkeley, whom you so uphold, would delight to honor; a man whom the worldlings of Boston hold in as much horror as the worldlings of ancient Athens did Socrates. They smile to hear their verdict confirmed from the other side of the Atlantic, by their censor, Harriet Martineau.

LETTERS, 1837

I had a (to me) very pleasant visit from Mr. Alcott. I saw him by the light of his own eyes. With me alone he is never the Messiah but one beautiful individuality and faithful soul. Then he seems really high and not merely a person of high pretensions. I think his "Sayings" are quite grand, though ofttimes too grandiloquent. I thought he bore my strictures with great sweetness for they must have seemed petty to him. — Tell him that Mr. Ripley verified at once my prophecy and said what I told him would be said about the Prometheus.

LETTERS, 1840

New England is now old enough, — some there have leisure enough, — to look at all this; and the consequence is a violent reaction, in a small minority, against a mode of culture that rears such fruits. They see that political freedom does not necessarily produce liberality of mind, nor freedom in church institutions — vital religion; and, seeing that these changes cannot be wrought from without inwards, they are trying to quicken the soul, that they may work from within outwards. Disgusted with the vulgarity of a commercial aristocracy, they become radicals; disgusted with the materialistic working of "rational" religion, they become mystics. They quarrel with all that is, because it is not spiritual enough. They would, perhaps, be patient if they thought this the mere sensuality of childhood in our nation, which it might outgrow; but they think that they see the evil widening, deepening, — not only debasing the life, but corrupting the thought of our people, and they feel that if they know not well what should be done, yet that the duty of every good man is to utter a protest against what is done amiss.

Is this protest undiscriminating? are these opinions crude? do these proceedings threaten to sap the bulwarks on which men at present depend? I confess it all, yet I see in these men promise of a better wisdom than in their opponents. Their hope for man is grounded on his destiny as an immortal soul, and not as a mere comfort-loving inhabitant of earth, or a subscriber to the social contract. It was not meant that the soul should cultivate the earth, but that the earth should educate and maintain the soul. Man is not made for society, but society is made for man. No institution can be good which does not tend to improve the individual. In these principles I have confidence so profound, that I am not afraid to trust those who hold them, despite their partial views, imperfectly developed characters, and frequent want of practical sagacity. I believe, if they have opportunity to state and discuss their opinions, they will gradually sift them, ascertain their grounds and aims with clearness, and do the work this country needs. I hope for them as for "the leaven that is hidden in the bushel of meal, till all be leavened." The leaven is not good by itself, neither is the meal; let them combine, and we shall yet have bread.

LETTERS, 1840

[Mr. Ripley] is quite bent on trying his experiment [Brook Farm]. I hope he may succeed; but as they were talking the other evening, I thought of the river, and all the pretty symbols the tide-mill presents, and felt if I could at all adjust the economics to the more simple procedure, I would far rather be the miller, hoping to attract by natural affinity some congenial baker, "und so weiter." However, one thing seems sure, that many persons will soon, somehow, somewhere, throw off a part, at least, of these terrible weights of the social contract, and see if they cannot lie more at ease in the lap of Nature. I do not feel the same interest in these plans, as if I had a firmer hold on life, but I listen with much pleasure to the good suggestions.

LETTERS, 1840

Utopia it is impossible to build up. At least, my hopes for our race on this one planet are more limited than those of most of my friends. I accept the limitations of human nature, and believe a wise acknowledgement of them one of the best conditions of progress. Yet every noble scheme, every poetic manifestation, prophesies to man his eventual destiny. And were not man ever more sanguine than facts at the moment justify, he would remain torpid, or be sunk in sensuality. It is on this ground that I sympathize with what is called the "Transcendental party," and that I feel their aim to be the true one. They acknowledge in the nature of man an arbiter for his deeds, — a standard transcending sense and time, — and are, in my view, the true utilitarians.

LETTERS, 1840

On Friday I came to Brook Farm. The first day or two here is desolate. You seem to belong to nobody, — to have a right to speak to nobody; but very soon you learn to take care of yourself, and then the freedom of the place is delightful.

It is fine to see how thoroughly Mr. and Mrs. R[ipley] act out, in their own persons, what they intend.

All Saturday I was off in the woods. In the evening we had a general conversation, opened by me, upon Education, in its largest sense, and on what we can do for ourselves and others. I took my usual ground: The aim is perfection; patience the road. The present object is to give ourselves and others a tolerable chance. Let us not be too ambitious in our hopes as to immediate results. Our lives should be considered as a tendency, an approximation only. Parents and teachers expect to do too much. They are not legislators, but only interpreters to the next generation. Soon, very soon, does the parent become merely the elder brother of his child; — a little wiser, it is to be hoped. _____ differed from me as to some things I said about the gradations of experience, — that "to be brought prematurely near perfect beings would chill and

87

discourage." He thought it would cheer and console. He spoke well, — with a youthful nobleness. _____ said "that the most perfect person would be the most impersonal" — philosophical bull that, I trow — "and, consequently, would impede us least from God." Mr. R. spoke admirably on the nature of loyalty. The people showed a good deal of the *sans-culotte* tendency in their manners, — throwing themselves on the floor, yawning, and going out when they had heard enough. Yet, as the majority differ from me, to begin with, — that being the reason this subject was chosen, — they showed, on the whole, more respect and interest than I had expected. As I am accustomed to deference, however, and need it for the boldness and animation which my part requires, I did not speak with as much force as usual. Still, I should like to have to face all this; it would have the same good effects that the Athenian assemblies had on the minds obliged to encounter them.

MEMOIRS

Saturday. Well, good-by, Brook Farm. I know more about this place than I did when I came; but the only way to be qualified for a judge of such an experiment would be to become an active, though unimpassioned, associate in trying it. Some good things are proven, and as for individuals, they are gainers . . . .

I have found myself here in the amusing position of a conservative. Even so is it with Mr. R. There are too many young people in proportion to the others. I heard myself saying, with a grave air, "Play out the play, gentles." Thus, from generation to generation, rises and falls the wave.

MEMOIRS

Here I have passed a very pleasant week. The tone of the society is much sweeter than when I was here a year ago. There is a pervading spirit of mutual tolerance and gentleness, with great sincerity. There is no longer a passion for grotesque freaks of liberty, but a disposition, rather, to study and enjoy the liberty of law. The great development of mind and character observable in several instances, persuades me that this state of things affords a fine studio for the soul-sculptor. To a casual observer it may seem as if there was not enough of character here to interest, because there are no figures sufficiently distinguished to be worth painting for the crowd; but there is enough of individuality in free play to yield instruction; and one might have, from a few months' residence here, enough of the human drama to feed thought for a long time.

MEMOIRS

Mr. Parker was a highly esteemed member of the Christian Unitarian body till, some four years since, he uttered himself with freedom on a few points, in a way distasteful to the majority. Part of the offence consisted in views expressed by him as to the nature of inspiration, and the facts of Bible history, in which he really differs from the majority; part in attacks upon abuses which he saw, or thought he saw, in the church to which he belonged, such as may be inferred from the heads of "The Pharisees," "Idolatry," &c.

Then arose a good deal of outcry which was well, for it called on Mr. Parker to explain himself, and give the multitude of hearers an opportunity to consider his arguments, and judge whether they coincided with his censures. He delivered many lectures to full and eager audiences, and, no doubt, where there existed in that community a tendency congenial with his, has been a principal agent in its development. At the same time, a very strong and wide dissent was manifested.

A tacit persecution followed on the part of the clergy, in which they were sustained by a part of the community. It was almost impossible for Mr. Parker to obtain an exchange with any pulpit. As to this, we think that a clergyman has a right to avoid uncongenial cooperation in this way, just as he has to decline uncongenial books, or uncongenial visitors, but we think also that it is unwise to exercise this right. 1st; because we all need uncongenial statements, and the view of the other side, to prevent the mind from becoming petrified and narrowed. Free air is needed, even if it does sometimes come harshly, sometimes sultry. 2d; it is the sure way to give the proscribed party influence. So it was in this case. The flock ran out of the fold to seek the wolf. Mr. Parker was invited to lecture every where, and the *meeting-house* was deserted for the lecture-room.

REVIEW OF THEODORE PARKER, THE EXCELLENCE OF GOODNESS

Mr. Parker is a man of vigorous abilities and extensive information. He writes in a forcible and full, but not diffuse, style. His great attraction for his hearers is his perfect frankness. He is willing to lay his mind completely open, without circumlocution or complaisance, and possesses the power of doing this adequately. What God sees, man may see and make what use of it he can. — He is no orator, but has a full and manly style of speaking commensurate with his matter. We do not find in Mr. Parker a depth of spiritual discernment, nor the poetic faculty. He is, as a mind, more broad than high or deep. Persons of far inferior mental development can see clearly fallacies in his estimate of facts in religious history. He is too combative for our taste; he loves to assail the false, or what he esteems to be such, as well as to declare truths. But his large ken and mental integrity entitle him to be heard. We doubt not that any agitation caused by him in the atmosphere will show, in its results, the purifying power of electricity. And we regret that, in the nineteenth century, "liberal Christians" should not be liberal enough cheerfully to allow an honorable mind free course, and fearlessly leave the result to God and His unfailing Agent, Time.

REVIEW OF THEODORE PARKER, *THE EXCELLENCE OF GOODNESS*

When Souls Meet

Margaret Fuller wanted more from her relationships than acceptance and mutual esteem, she desired a meeting of souls, "a pilgrimage towards a common shrine." Such high expectations were often thwarted, leaving her lonely and depressed. But if others, such as Emerson, worshiped Truth, Fuller worshiped Love, and she sought it in her friendships with women as well as with men. Perhaps she found the kind of love she was looking for in her marriage to Giovanni Ossoli, a young Italian count she met in Rome and with whom she had a child; and yet, as she says, "our relation only covers a part of my life."

When souls meet direct and all secret thoughts are laid open, we shall need no forbearance, no prevention, no care-taking of any kind. Love will be pure light, and each action simple, — too simple to be noble. But there will not be always so much to pardon in ourselves and others. Yesterday we had at my class a conversation on Faith. Deeply true things were said and felt. But to-day the virtue has gone out of me; I have accepted all, and yet there will come these hours of weariness, — weariness of human nature in myself and others . . . . To speak with open heart and "tongue affectionate and true," — to enjoy real repose and the consciousness of a thorough mutual understanding in the presence of friends when we do meet, is what is needed . . . . In peace, in stillness that permits the soul to flow, beneath the open sky, I would see those I love.

LETTERS, 1842

We meet — at least those who are true to their instincts meet — a succession of persons through our lives, all of whom have some peculiar errand to us. There is an outer circle, whose existence we perceive, but with whom we stand in no real relation. They tell us the news, they act on us in the offices of society, they show us kindness and aversion; but their influence does not penetrate; we are nothing to them, nor they to us, except as a part of the world's furniture. Another circle, within this, are dear and near to us. We know them and of what kind they are. They are to us not mere facts, but intelligible thoughts of the divine mind. We like to see how they are unfolded; we like to meet them and part from them; we like their action upon us and the pause that succeeds and enables us to appreciate its quality. Often we leave them on our path, and return no more, but we bear them in our memory, tales which have been told, and whose meaning has been felt.

AUTOBIOGRAPHICAL SKETCH

This week I have not read any book, nor once walked in the woods and field. I meant to give its days to setting outward things in order, and its evenings to writing. But, I know not how it is, I can never simplify my life; always so many ties, so many claims! However, soon the winter winds will chant matins and vespers, which may make my house a cell, and in a snowy veil enfold me for my prayer. If I cannot dedicate myself this time, I will not expect it again . . . .

Why is it that the religion of my nature is so much hidden from my peers? why do they question me, who never question them? why persist to regard as a meteor an orb of assured hope? Can no soul know me wholly? shall I never know the deep delight of gratitude to any but the All-Knowing?

LETTERS, 1840

I like to be in your [Emerson's] library when you are out of it. It seems a sacred place. I came here to find a book, that I might feel more life and be worthy to sleep, but there is so much soul here I do not need a book. When I come to yourself, I cannot receive you, and you cannot give yourself; it does not profit. But when I cannot find you the beauty and permanence of your life come to me.

"She (Poesie) has ascended from the depths of a nature, and only by a similar depth, shall she be apprehended!" — I want to say while I am feeling it, what I have often (not always) great pleasure in feeling — how long it must be, before I am able to meet you. — I see you — and fancied it nearer than it was, you were right in knowing the contrary.

How much, much more I would fain say and cannot. I am too powerfully drawn while with you, and cannot advance a step, but when away I have learned something. Not yet to be patient and faithful and holy however, but only have taken off the shoes, to tread the holy ground. I shall often depart through the ranges of manifold being, but as often return to where I am tonight.

LETTERS, 1841

My dear friend, We shall never meet on these subjects while one atom of our proper individualities remains. Yet let me say a few words more on my side. The true love has no need of illusion: it is too deeply prophetic in its nature to be baffled or chilled, much less changed by the accidents of time. We are sure that what we love is living, though the ruins of old age have fallen upon the shrine. The "blank gray" upon the hallowed locks, the dimmed eye, the wasted cheek cannot deceive us. Neither can the diminution of vital fire and force, the scantiness of thought, the loss of grace, wit, fancy and springing enthusiasm, for it was none of these we loved, but the true self, that particular emanation from God which was made to correspond with that which we are, to teach it, to learn from it, to torture it, to enchant it, to deepen and at last to satisfy our wants. You go upon the idea that we must love most the most beauteous, but this is not so. We love most that which by working most powerfully on our peculiar nature awakens most deeply and constantly in us the idea of beauty. Where we have once seen clearly what is fit for us, if only in the glance of an eye we cannot forget it, nor can any change in the form where we have seen it deceive us. We know that it will appear again and clothe the scene with new and greater beauty.

LETTERS, 1841

Waldo and I went to walk to Walden pond, as usual, and staid till near sunset on the water's brink beneath the pines. It was a very lovely afternoon, great happy clouds floating, a light breeze rippling the water to our feet: it was altogether sweet, and not out of memory, as is too often the case between us, but from the present moment and to be remembered. We go but very little way on our topics, just touch and taste and leave the cup not visibly shallower. Waldo said once his were short flights from bough to bough, and so it is not up into the blue. I feel more at home with him constantly, but we do not act powerfully on one another. He is a much better companion than formerly, for once he would talk obstinately through the walk, but now we can be silent and see things together. We talked on the subject of his late letter, the threatenings of the time which come to so little, and of some individual cases where Sorrow is still the word, of those who began with such high resolve.

JOURNAL, 1842

I feel that the darkest hue on my own lot is that I have neither children, nor yet am the parent of beautiful works by which the thought of my life might be represented to another generation. Yet even this is not dark to me, though it sometimes makes me pensive. — I have not lived my own life, neither loved my own love, my strength, my sympathies have been given to others, their lives are my aims. If here I could call nothing my own, it has led me to penetrate deeper into the thought which pervades all. I have not been led to limit my thoughts to a span, nor fix my affections with undue order on some one set of objects. So all things are equalized at last. — I cannot help regretting sometimes that I can do so little for any one, so little for my nearest and dearest to soothe their pains, or remove obstacles from their path. Yet is *that little* not often to be met with. I can say from the depth of my heart, never cease to hope and trust if you deserve you will at last be satisfied.

LETTERS, 1842

The sexes should not only correspond to and appreciate, but prophesy to one another. In individual instances this happens. Two persons love in one another the future good which they aid one another to unfold. This is imperfectly or rarely done in the general life. Man has gone but little way; now he is waiting to see whether woman can keep step with him, but instead of calling out, like a good brother, "you can do it, if you only think so," or impersonally; "any one can do what he tries to do"; he often discourages with school-boy brag: "Girls can't do that; girls can't play ball." But let any one defy their taunts, break through and be brave and secure, they rend the air with shouts.

WOMAN IN THE NINETEENTH CENTURY

This golden afternoon I walked with Waldo to the hemlocks. There we sat down and staid till near sunset. He read me verses. — Dichtung und Wahrheit (poetry and truth) is certainly the name for his life, for he does not care for facts, except so far as the immortal essence can be distilled from them. He has little sympathy with mere life: does not seem to see the plants grow, merely that he may rejoice in their energy.

We got to talking, as we almost always do, on Man and Woman, and Marriage. — W. took his usual ground. Love is only phenomenal, a contrivance of nature, in her circular motion. Man, in proportion as he is completely unfolded is man and woman by turns. The soul knows nothing of marriage, in the sense of a permanent union between two personal existences. The soul is married to each new thought as it enters into it. If this thought puts on the form of man or woman, if it last you seventy years, what then? There is but one love, that for the Soul of all Souls, let it put on what cunning disguises it will, still at last you find yourself lonely, — *the Soul.*

There seems to be no end to these conversations: they always leave us both where they found us, but we enjoy them, for we often get a good expression.

JOURNAL, 1842

It is so true that a woman may be in love with a woman, and a man with a man. It is so pleasant to be sure of it because undoubtedly it is the same love that we shall feel when we are angels. . . . It is regulated by the same law as that of love between persons of different sexes, only it is purely intellectual and spiritual, unprofaned by any mixture of lower instincts, undisturbed by any need of consulting temporal interests, its law is the desire of the spirit to realize a whole which makes it seek in another being for what it finds not in itself. Thus the beautiful seeks the strong, and the strong the beautiful, the mute seeks the eloquent. . . . How natural is [my] love . . . for Anna Barker. I loved Anna for a time I think with as much passion as I was then strong enough to feel — Her face was always gleaming before me, her voice was echoing in my ear, all poetic thoughts clustered round the dear image. This love was a key which unlocked for me many a treasure which I still possess, it was the carbuncle (emblematic gem) which cast light into many of the darkest caverns of human nature.

JOURNAL, 1842

At present, it skills not, I am able to take the superior views of life, and my place in it: but I know the deep yearnings of the heart and the bafflings of time will again be felt, and then I shall long for some dear hand to hold. But I shall never forget that my curse is nothing compared with that of those who have entered into those relations but not made them real: who only *seem* husbands, wives, and friends. . . .

My head aches today, I can scarce do any thing.

Yet have been reading the books of Confucius with great edification. It seems to me my mind acts in a different way when I have this heat and pressure on the top of the head from what it does at other times.

Confucius, like Jesus, had one beloved disciple, one who understood him, the great the virtuous Hwuy. He who never discussed, never questioned but understood all, who was happy while his food was a dry crust, his habitation in a mean lane; He who if you gave him one point always had ten or the whole while the other disciples if you gave them one point only had two or the opposite. Yet Confucius says,

"Alas no one knows me! Isze-Kurny said, how is it that you are not known, Sir. Confucius replied, I repine not at heaven: I grumble not with men; I study the inferior branches of learning and advance to a clear knowledge of the superior. It is only heaven that knows me."

Yes, it is only love, that heaven on earth, that can make any mortal cease for a moment to be lonely: that divines, and its knowledge is divine. Sages must be alone children and lovers are not. But it is no easier to be always a lover than always child: so the soul of the mortal must often be alone.

JOURNAL, 1844

The lot of woman is sad. She is constituted to expect and need a happiness that cannot exist on earth. She must stifle such aspirations within her secret heart, and fit herself, as well as she can, for a life of resignations and consolations.

She will be very lonely while living with her husband. She must not expect to open her heart to him fully, or that, after marriage, he will be capable of the refined service of love. The man is not born for the woman, only the woman for the man. "Men cannot understand the hearts of women." The life of woman must be outwardly a well-intentioned, cheerful dissimulation of her real life.

Naturally, the feelings of the mother, at the birth of a female child, resemble those of the Paraguay woman, described by Southey as lamenting in such heart-breaking tones that her mother did not kill her the hour she was born.

WOMAN IN THE NINETEENTH CENTURY

The man furnishes the house; the woman regulates it. Their relation is one of mutual esteem, mutual dependence. Their talk is of business, their affection shows itself by practical kindness. They know that life goes more smoothly and cheerfully to each for the other's aid; they are grateful and content. The wife praises her husband as a "good provider"; the husband, in return, compliments her as a "capital housekeeper." This relation is good, as far as it goes.

Next comes a closer tie, which takes the two forms, either of mutual idolatry, or of intellectual companionship. The first, we suppose, is to no one a pleasing subject of contemplation. The parties weaken and narrow one another; they lock the gate against all the glories of the universe, that they may live in a cell together. To themselves they seem the only wise, to all others steeped in infatuation; the gods smile as they look forward to the crisis of cure; to men, the woman seems an unlovely syren; to women, the man an effeminate boy.

The other form, of intellectual companionship, has become more and more frequent. Men engaged in public life, literary men, and artists, have often found in their wives companions and confidants in thought no less than in feeling. And as the intellectual development of woman has spread wider and risen higher, they have, not unfrequently, shared the same employment.

WOMAN IN THE NINETEENTH CENTURY

The fourth and highest grade of marriage union is the religious, which may be expressed as pilgrimage toward a common shrine. This includes the others: home sympathies and household wisdom, for these pilgrims must know how to assist each other along the dusty way; intellectual communion, for how sad it would be on such a journey to have a companion to whom you could not communicate thoughts and aspirations as they sprang to life; who would have no feeling for the prospects that open, more and more glorious as we advance; who would never see the flowers that may be gathered by the most industrious traveller! It must include all these.

WOMAN IN THE NINETEENTH CENTURY

The world seems to go so strangely wrong! The bad side triumphs; the blood and tears of the generous flow in vain. I assist at many saddest scenes, and suffer for those whom I knew not before. Those whom I knew and loved, — who, if they had triumphed, would have opened for me an easier, broader, higher-mounting road, — are every day more and more involved in earthly ruin. Eternity is with us, but there is much darkness and bitterness in this portion of it. A baleful star rose on my birth, and its hostility, I fear, will never be disarmed while I walk below.

LETTERS, 1849

You say no secret can be kept in the civilized world and I suppose not long, but it is very important to me to keep this, for the present, if possible, and by and by to have the mode of disclosure at my option. For this, I have made the cruellest sacrifices; it will, indeed, be just like the rest, if they are made of none effect.

After I wrote to you I went to Rieti. The weather was mild when I set out, but by the fatality that has attended me throughout, in the night changed to a cold, unknown in Italy and remained so all the time I staid. There was, as is common in Italy, no fireplace except in the kitchen. I suffered much in my room with its brick floor, and windows through which came the cold wind freely. My darling did not suffer, because he was a little swaddled child like this and robed in wool beside, but I did very much. When I first took him in my arms he made no sound but leaned his head against my bosom, and staid so, he seemed to say how could you abandon me, what I felt you will know only when you have your own . . . . You speak of my being happy; all the solid happiness I have known has been at times when he went to sleep in my arms.

LETTERS, 1849

Should I never return, — and sometimes I despair of doing so, it seems so far off, so difficult, I am caught in such a net of ties here, — if ever you know of my life here, I think you will only wonder at the constancy with which I have sustained myself; the degree of profit to which, amid great difficulties, I have put the time, at least in the way of observation. Meanwhile, love me all you can; let me feel, that, amid the fearful agitations of the world, there are pure hands, with healthful, even pulse, stretched out toward me, if I claim their grasp . . . .

Then Rome is being destroyed; her glorious oaks; her villas, haunts of sacred beauty, that seemed the possession of the world forever, — the villa of Raphael, the villa of Albani, home of Winkelmann, and the best expression of the ideal of modern Rome, and so may other sanctuaries of beauty, — all must perish, lest a foe should level his musket from their shelter. *I* could not, could not!

I know not, dear friend, whether I ever shall get home across that great ocean, but here in Rome I shall no longer wish to live. O, Rome, *my* country! could I imagine that the triumph of what I held dear was to heap such desolation on thy head!

LETTERS, 1849

My love for Ossoli is most pure and tender, nor has any one, except little children or mother, ever loved me as genuinely as he does. To you, dear William I was obliged to make myself known; others have loved me with a mixture of fancy and enthusiasm excited by my talent at embellishing subjects. He loves me from simple affinity; he loves to be with me, and serve and soothe me. Our relation covers only a part of my life, but I do not perceive that it interferes with anything I ought to have or be; I do not feel any way constrained or limited or that I have made any sacrifice . . . . You speak as if I might return to America without him. I thought of it at one time, knowing it would be very trying for him to go with me, that when I first am with my former friends, he may have many lonely hours. Beside he had then an employment in Rome and we needed the money. I thought I would go and either write for him to come to me, or return to Italy. But now that cannot be. He could not at present reenter Rome without danger; he is separated from his employment and his natural friends, nor is any career open for him in Italy at present. Then I could not think of taking away the child for several months; his heart is fixed on the child as fervently as mine. Then it would not only be very strange and sad to me to be without his love and care for weeks and months, but I should feel very anxious about him under present circumstances. I trust we shall find means to make the voyage together and remain together. In our country he will have for resources, his walks and quiet communings with nature, which is always so great a part of his life; he will have the child, and I think my family, expecially my mother, will love him very dearly and he will be learning the language with them. I suppose I must myself be engaged in the old unhealthy way, life will probably be a severe struggle. I hope I shall be able to live through it, and not neglect my child, nor Ossoli. He has suffered enough; it has ploughed furrows in his life since first we met. He has done all he could and cannot blame himself. Our destiny is sad; we must brave it as we can. I hope we shall always feel mutual tenderness, and Ossoli has a simple child-like piety that will make it easier for him.

LETTERS, 1849

Sad are the catastrophes of friendships, for they are mostly unequal, and it is rare that more than one party keeps true to the original covenant. Happy the survivor if in losing his friend, he loses not the idea of friendship, nor can be made to believe, because those who were once to him the angels of his life, sustaining the aspiration of his nobler nature, and calming his soul by the gleams of pure beauty that for a time were seen in their deeds, in their desires, unexpectedly grieve the spirit, and baffle the trust which had singled them out as types of excellence amid a sullied race, by infirmity of purpose, shallowness of heart and mind, selfish absorption or worldly timidity, that there is no such thing as true intimacy, as harmonious development of mind by mind, two souls prophesying to one another, two minds feeding one another, two human hearts sustaining and pardoning one another.

BETTINE BRENTANO AND HER FRIEND GUNDERODE

Without full confidence no friendship can subsist, none without generosity, without unwearied sympathy, and the modesty that permits, when suffering, to receive this balm. But also none can subsist and grow, without mutual stimulus, without an infinite promise, a stern demand of excellence from either side, and revelations of thoughts, not only hoarded from the past, but constantly new-born from intercourse between the two natures. There must be faith in one another, action upon one another, love, patiently to wait for one another.

BETTINE BRENTANO AND HER FRIEND GUNDERODE

The Magic Mirror

Margaret Fuller was a pioneer in many ways — as a feminist and public intellectual, to be sure, but also as the editor of the Dial magazine and as a columnist for a major New York newspaper reviewing literature, drama, and music. In this she helped to shape artistic tastes and to establish both the canon of American literature and the criteria by which it was to be judged. Fuller promoted artistic expression and critical engagement with the arts as necessary to the spiritual and moral growth of the individual, the nation, and the human race.

For the arts are no luxury, no mere ornament and stimulus to a civic and complicated existence, as the worldling and the ascetic alike delight in representing them to be, but the herbarium in which are preserved the fairest flowers of man's existence, the magic mirror by whose aid all its phases are interpreted, the circle into which the various spirits of the elements may be invoked and made to reveal the secret they elsewhere manifest only in large revolutions of time; and what philosophy, with careful steps and anxious ear, has long sought in vain, is oftentimes revealed at once by a flash from this torch.

CANOVA

The critic is beneath the maker, but is his needed friend. What tongue could speak but to an intelligent ear, and every noble work demands its critic. The richer the work, the more severe would be its critic; the larger its scope, the more comprehensive must be his power of scrutiny.

The critic is not a base caviller, but the younger brother of genius. Next to invention is the power of interpreting invention; next to beauty the power of appreciating beauty.

And of making others appreciate it; for the universe is a scale of infinite gradation, and below the very highest, every step is explanation down to the lowest. Religion, in the two modulations of poetry and music, descends through an infinity of waves to the lowest abysses of human nature. Nature is the literature and art of the divine mind; human literature and art the criticism on that; and they, too, find their criticism within their own sphere.

The critic, then, should be not merely a poet, not merely a philosopher, not merely an observer, but tempered of all three. If he criticize the poem, he must want nothing of what constitutes the poet, except the power of creating forms and speaking in music. He must have as good an eye and as fine a sense; but if he had as fine an organ for expression also, he would make the poem instead of judging it. He must be inspired by the philosopher's spirit of inquiry and need of generalization, but he must not be constrained by the hard cemented masonry of method to which philosophers are prone. And he must have the organic acuteness of the observer, with a love of ideal perfection, which forbids him to be content with mere beauty of details in the work or the comment upon the work.

A SHORT ESSAY ON CRITICS

Life is living, and art, European art, lives in the opera and ballet. For us we have nothing of our own, for the same reason that in literature, a few pale buds is all that we yet can boast of native growth, because we have no national character of sufficient fulness and simplicity to demand it. There is nothing particular to be said, as yet, but everything to be done and observed. Why should we be babbling? let us see, let us help the plant to grow; when it is once grown, then paint it, then describe it. We earn our brown bread, but we beg our cake; yet we want some, for we are children still.

ENTERTAINMENTS OF THE PAST WINTER

If New England thinks, it is about money, social reform, and theology. If she has a way of speaking peculiarly her own, it is the lecture. But the lecture, though of such banyan growth among us, seems not to bespeak any deep or permanent tendency. Intellectual curiosity and sharpness are the natural traits of a colony overrun with things to be done, to be seen, to be known from a parent country possessing a rich and accumulating treasure from centuries of civilized life. Lectures upon every possible topic are the short business way taken by a business people to find out what there is to be known, but to *know* in such ways cannot be hoped, unless the suggestions thus received are followed up by private study, thought, conversation. This, no doubt, is done in some degree, but chiefly by the young, not yet immersed in the stream of things. Let any one listen in an omnibus, or at a boarding house, to the conversation suggested by last night's lecture, see the composure with which the greatest blunders and most unfounded assertions are heard and assented to, and he will be well convinced how little the subject has occupied the minds of the smart and curious audience, and feel less admiration at the air of devout attention which pervades an Odeon assembly. Not that it is unmeaning, something they learn; but it is to be feared just enough to satisfy, not stimulate the mind. It is an entertainment which leaves the hearer too passive. One that appealed to the emotions would enter far more deeply and pervasively into the life, than these addressed to the understanding, a faculty already developed out of all proportion among this people.

ENTERTAINMENTS OF THE PAST WINTER

Waldo had got through with his tedious prose, and to day he got into the mood to finish his poem. Just at night he came into the red room to read the passage he had inserted. This is to me the loveliest way to live that we have. I wish it would be so always that I could live in the red room, and Waldo be stimulated by the fine days to write poems and come the rainy days to read them to me. My time to go to him is late in the evening. Then I go knock at the library door, and we have our long word walk through the growths of things with glimmers of light from the causes of things. Afterward, W. goes out and walks beneath the stars to compose himself for his pillow, and I open the window, and sit in the great red chair to watch them.

JOURNAL, 1842

With the first rosy streak, I was out among my Indian neighbors, whose lodges honey-combed the beautiful beach, that curved away in long, fair outline on either side the house. They were already on the alert, the children creeping out from beneath the blanket door of the lodge; the women pounding corn in their rude mortars, the young men playing on their pipes. I had been much amused, when the strain proper to the Winnebago courting flute was played to me on another instrument, at any one fancying it a melody; but now, when I heard the notes in their true tone and time, I thought it not unworthy comparison, in its graceful sequence, and the light flourish, at the close, with the sweetest bird-songs; and this, like the bird-song, is only practised to allure a mate. The Indian, become a citizen and a husband, no more thinks of playing the flute than one of the "settled down" members of our society would of choosing the "purple light of love" as dye-stuff for a surtout.

SUMMER ON THE LAKES

Poetry is not a superhuman or supernatural gift. It is, on the contrary, the fullest and therefore most completely natural expression of what is human. It is that of which the rudiments lie in every human breast, but developed to a more complete existence than the obstructions of daily life permit, clothed in an adequate form, domesticated in nature by the use of apt images, the perception of grand analogies, and set to the music of the spheres for the delight of all who have ears to hear. We have uttered these remarks, which may, to many of our readers, seem truisms, for the sake of showing that our definition of poetry is large enough to include all kinds of excellence. It includes not only the great bards, but the humblest minstrels. The great bards bring to light the more concealed treasures, gems which centuries have been employed in forming and which it is their office to reveal, polish, and set for the royal purposes of man; the wandering minstrel with his lighter but beautiful office calls the attention of men to the meaning of the flowers, which also is hidden from the careless eye, though they have grown and bloomed in full sight of all who chose to look. All the poets are the priests of Nature, though the greatest are also the prophets of the manhood of man. For, when fully grown, the life of man must be all poetry; each of his thoughts will be a key to the treasures of the universe; each of his acts a revelation of beauty, his language will be music, and his habitual presence will overflow with more energy and inspire with a nobler rapture than do the fullest strains of lyric poetry now.

Meanwhile we need poets; men more awakened to the wonders of life, and gifted more or less with a power to express what they see, and to all who possess, in any degree, those requisites we offer and we owe welcome and tribute, whether the place of their song be in the Pantheon, from which issue the grand decrees of immortal thought, or by the fireside, where hearts need kindling and eyes need clarifying by occasional drops of nectar in their tea.

But this — this alone we claim, and can welcome none who cannot present this title to our hearing; that the vision be genuine, the expression spontaneous. No imposition upon our young fellow citizens of pinchbeck for gold! they must have the true article, and pay the due intellectual price, or they will wake from a life-long dream of folly to find themselves beggars.

AMERICAN LITERATURE

Of this great life which has risen from the stalk and the leaf into bud, and will, in the course of this age, be in full flower, Beethoven is the last and greatest exponent. His music is felt by every soul whom it affects to be the explanation of the past, and the prophecy of the future. It contains the thoughts of the time. A dynasty of great men preceded him, each of whom made conquests and accumulated treasures which prepared the way for his successor. Bach, Handel, Haydn, Mozart, were corner-stones of the glorious temple. Who shall succeed Beethoven? A host of musicians full of talent, even of genius, live now he is dead, but the greatest among them is confessed by all men to be but of Lilliputian size compared with this demi-god. Indeed, it should be so! — As copious draughts of soul have been given to the earth as she can quaff for a century or more. — Disciples and critics must follow to gather up the gleanings of the golden grain . . . .

The life of a Beethoven is written in his works, and all that can be told of his life beside is but as marginal notes on that broad page. Yet since we have these notes, it is pleasant to have them in harmony with the page. The acts and words of Beethoven are what we should expect, noble, leonine, impetuous, but tender. His faults are the faults of one so great that he found few paths wide enough for his tread and knew not how to moderate it. They are not faults in themselves, but only in relation to the men who surrounded him. Among his peers he would not have had faults. As it is they hardly deserve the name.

REVIEW OF *THE LIFE OF BEETHOVEN*

Oh! pain-staking friends, shut your books, clear your minds from artificial nonsense, and feel that only by spirit can spirit be discerned. Dante, like each other great one, took the stuff that lay around him and wove it to a garment of light. It is not by raveling that you will best appreciate its tissue or design. It is not by studying out the petty strifes or external relations of his time that you can become acquainted with the thought of Dante. To him these things were only soil in which to plant himself — figures by which to dramatize and evolve his ideas. Would you learn him, go listen in the forest of human passions to all the terrible voices he heard with a tormented but never to be deafened ear; go down into the hells where each excess that mars the harmony of nature is punished by the sinner finding no food except from his own harvest; pass through the purgatories of speculation, of struggling hope, and faith, never quite quenched, but smoldering often and long beneath the ashes. Soar if thou canst, but if thou canst not, clear thine eye to see this great eagle soar into the higher region where forms arrange themselves for stellar dance and spheral melody, and thought, with constantly accelerated motion, raises itself in a spiral which can end only in the heart of the Supreme.

ITALY

The volume before us shares the charms of Hawthorne's earlier tales; the only difference being that his range of subjects is a little wider. There is the same gentle and sincere companionship with Nature, the same delicate but fearless scrutiny of the secrets of the heart, the same serene independence of petty and artificial restrictions, whether on opinions or conduct, the same familiar, yet pensive sense of the spiritual or demoniacal influences that haunt the palpable life and common walks of men, not by many apprehended except in results. We have here to regret that Hawthorne, at this stage of his mind's life, lay no more decisive hand upon the apparition — brings it no nearer than in former days. — We had hoped that we should see, no more as in a glass darkly, but face to face. Still, still brood over his page the genius of revery and the nonchalance of Nature, rather than the ardent earnestness of the human soul which feels itself born not only to see and disclose, but to understand and interpret such things. Hawthorne intimates and suggests, but he does not lay bare the mysteries of our being.

REVIEW OF *MOSSES FROM AN OLD MANSE*

That such a genius is to rise and work in this hemisphere we are confident; equally so that scarce the first faint streaks of that day's dawn are yet visible. It is sad for those that foresee, to know they may not live to share its glories, yet it is sweet, too, to know that every act and word, uttered in the light of that foresight, may tend to hasten or ennoble its fulfillment.

That day will not rise till the fusion of races among us is more complete. It will not rise till this nation shall attain sufficient moral and intellectual dignity to prize moral and intellectual, no less highly than political, freedom, not till, the physical resources of the country being explored, all its regions studded with towns, broken by the plow, netted together by railways and telegraph lines, talent shall be left at leisure to turn its energies upon the higher department of man's existence. Nor then shall it be seen till from the leisurely and yearning soul of that riper time national ideas shall take birth, ideas craving to be clothed in a thousand fresh and original forms.

Without such ideas all attempts to construct a national literature must end in abortions like the monster of Frankenstein, things with forms, and the instincts of forms, but soulless, and therefore revolting. We cannot have expression till there is something to be expressed.

AMERICAN LITERATURE

A man who feels within his mind some spark of genius, or a capacity for the exercises of talent, should consider himself as endowed with a sacred commission. He is the natural priest, the shepherd of the people. He must raise his mind as high as he can toward the heaven of truth, and try to draw up with him those less gifted by nature with ethereal lightness. If he does not so, but rather employs his powers to flatter them in their poverty, and to hinder aspiration by useless words, and a mere seeming of activity, his sin is great, he is false to God, and false to man . . . .

If only as a representative of the claims of individual culture in a nation which tends to lay such stress on artificial organization and external results, Mr. Emerson would be invaluable here. History will inscribe his name as a father of the country, for he is one who pleads her cause against herself.

EMERSON'S ESSAYS

Every day I rose and attended to the many little calls which are always on me, and which have been more of late. Then, about eleven, I would sit down to write, at my window,

close to which is the apple-tree lately full of blossoms, and now of yellow birds. Opposite me was Del Sarto's Madonna; behind me Silenus, holding in his arms the infant Pan. I felt very content with my pen, my daily bouquet, and my yellow birds. About five I would go out and walk till dark; then would arrive my proofs, like crabbed old guardians, coming to tea every night. So passed each day. The 23rd of May, my birth-day, about one o'clock, I wrote the last line of my little book [*Summer On the Lakes*]; then I went to Mount Auburn, and walked gently among the graves.

LETTERS, 1844

Two high claims our writer can vindicate on the attention of his contemporaries. One from his sincerity. You have his thought just as it found place in the life of his own soul. Thus, however near or relatively distant its approximation to absolute truth, its action on you cannot fail to be healthful. It is a part of the free air.

He belongs to that band of whom there may be found a few in every age, and who now in known human history may be counted by hundreds, who worship the one God only, the God of Truth. They worship, not saints, nor creeds, nor churches, nor reliques, nor idols in any form. The mind is kept open to truth, and life only valued as a tendency toward it. This must be illustrated by acts and words of love, purity and intelligence. Such are the salt of the earth; let the minutest crystal of that salt be willingly by us held in solution.

The other is through that part of his life, which, if sometimes obstructed or chilled by the critical intellect, is yet the prevalent and the main source of his power. It is that by which he imprisons his hearer only to free him again as a "liberating God" (to use his own words). But indeed let us use them altogether, for none other, ancient or modern, can more worthily express how, making present to us the courses and destinies of nature, he invests himself with her serenity and animates us with her joy.

EMERSON'S ESSAYS

For all the tides of life that flow within me, I am dumb and ineffectual, when it comes to casting my thought into a form. No old one suits me. If I could invent one, it seems to me the pleasure of creation would make it possible for me to write. What shall I do, dear friend? I want force to be either a genius or a character. One should be either private or public. I love best to be a woman; but womanhood is at present too straitly-bounded to give me scope. At hours, I live truly as a woman; at others, I should stifle; as, on the other hand, I should palsy, when I would play the artist.

LETTERS, N.D.

Suggested Reading

Numerous anthologies of Margaret Fuller's writings are available in paperback editions. Complete texts are available online through Google Books. Many biographies of Margaret Fuller have appeared in recent years — the most detailed and balanced account is Charles Capper's two-volume work. Additional information about Fuller's life and works are available at numerous websites, particularly those listed below.

ANTHOLOGIES

Margaret Fuller, *The Essential Margaret Fuller*, Jeffrey Steele, ed., Rutgers University Press, 1992.

————, *The Portable Margaret Fuller*, Mary Kelley, ed., Penguin, 1995.

————, *The Woman and the Myth: Margaret Fuller's Life and Writings*, Bell Gale Chevigny, ed., Northeastern University Press, 1994.

BIOGRAPHIES

Charles Capper, *Margaret Fuller: An American Romantic Life, Vol. 1: The Private Years*, Oxford University Press, 1992.

————, *Margaret Fuller: An American Romantic Life, Vol. 2: The Public Years*, Oxford University Press, 2007.

Meg McGavran Murray, *Margaret Fuller: Wandering Pilgrim*, University of Georgia Press, 2008.

Joan Von Mehren, *Minerva and the Muse: A Life of Margaret Fuller*, University of Massachusetts Press, 1994.

CRITICAL INTERPRETATIONS

Margaret Vanderhaar Allen, *The Achievement of Margaret Fuller,* Pennsylvania State University Press, 1979.

Jeffery Steele, *Transfiguring America: Myth, Ideology, and Mourning in Margaret Fuller's Writing,* University of Missouri Press, 2001.

WEBSITES

The American Transcendentalism Web:
www.vcu.edu/engweb/transcendentalism/authors/fuller

The Dictionary of Unitarian Universalist Biography:
www25.uua.org/uuhs/duub/articles/margaretfuller.html

The Margaret Fuller Society:
http://mendota.english.wisc.edu/~jasteele

Transcendentalist Spirituality
www.transcendentalistspirituality.com

The Transcendentalists:
www.transcendentalists.com/margaret_fuller.html